D1826080

Bon=Mots

OF

SYDNEY SMITH

AND

R. BRINSLEY SHERIDAN

EDITED BY

WALTER JERROLD

WITH GROTESQUES BY

AUBREY BEARDSLEY

Copyright © 2011 Read Books Ltd.
This book is copyright and may not be
reproduced or copied in any way without
the express permission of the publisher in writing

British Library Cataloguing-in-Publication Data
A catalogue record for this book is available from
the British Library

Sydney Smith

Sydney Smith was born on 3rd June 1771 in Woodford, Essex, England.

Smith was educated at Winchester College, where he greatly distinguished himself, rising to the position of school captain. In fact, he and his brother were so recognised for thier all-round abilities that their school fellows signed a round-robin "refusing to try for the college prizes if the Smiths were allowed to contend for them anymore".

In 1789, upon leaving Winchester College, he became a scholar at New College, Oxford. He received a fellowship from the college and finally obtained his Master of Arts degree in 1796. Smith's intention was to go on to read for the bar, but his father refused and compelled him to join the clergy. He was ordained at Oxford in 1796 and became the curate of the village of Netheravon, near Amesbury in Salisbury Plain. The squire of the parish engaged Smith to tutor his son and the pair went to Edinburgh to study. While his pupil attended lectures, Smith studied moral philosophy, medicine, and chemistry.

Smith's first book 'Six Sermons, preached in Charlotte Street Chapel, Edinburgh' was published in 1800. He married Catharine Amelia Pybus in the same year and the couple settled in Edinburgh. While there, he helped set up the *Edinburgh Review* and became its first editor in 1802. He continued to write articles for the review for the next quarter of the century which were a key element to the publication's success.

Smith left Scotland in 1803 and relocated to London. He became well known as a preacher, lecturer, and society figure, and he often preached to huge crowds in Berkeley Chapel, Mayfair.. He lectured at the Royal Institution on moral philosophy and promoted progressive values such as the education of women and the abolition of slavery. He often destroyed paper copies of his lectures after they had served their purpose but his wife rescued some of the charred manuscripts and published them as 'Elementary Sketches of Moral Philosophy' in 1850.

His most famous work is *Peter Plymley's Letters* (1892) in

which he deals with the subject of Catholic emancipation, ridiculing the opposition of the country clergy.

Smith continued his career in the church, preaching in Yorkshire for twenty years and being appointed to a residentiary canonry at St Paul's Cathedral in 1831.

He is remembered as a fine wit and humourist, and is often quoted in English literary life. Smith died on 22nd February 1845.

Sydney Smith.

" *Wit makes its own welcome, and levels all distinctions.*" —EMERSON.

" *Blockheads, with reason, wicked wits abhor.*" —

" *The rays of wit gild wheresoe'er they strike.*" —
STILLINGWORTH.

" *Often it consisteth in one knows not what, and springeth up one can hardly tell how.*" —BARROW.

" *Not in vain hath he lived, whose beneficent mirth Hath lightened the frowns and the furrows of earth.*" —

" *While we're quaffing,
Let's have laughing—
Who the devil cares for more !*" —

" *Man could direct his way by plain reason, and support life by tasteless food ; but God has given him wit and flavour, laughter and perfume, to enliven the days of man's pilgrimage, and to charm his pained steps over the burning marl.*" —SYDNEY SMITH.

INTRODUCTION.

SYDNEY SMITH.

"WHEN Philip of Macedon was king," says Dr Doran, "there was a club of wits in Athens which met once a week—not in a tavern, but in the temple of Hercules. They had such a favourable opinion of their own powers, that they chronicled all their own jokes ; and kings sent to borrow the book—*The Book of the Sixty*." In after years, any Athenian telling a "good story" was in danger of hearing that it was "one of the Sixty," even as, to-day, in similar circumstances, we are ready to cry "Joe Miller" or, less politely, "chestnuts." And so it is that when a good story, a witty retort, a *bon-mot* is to be repeated, it is put down to the reigning wit. How many stories, for example, are credited indiscriminately to Sydney Smith, Sheridan, Douglas Jerrold, Theodore Hook, Samuel Foote, and others. Absolute certainty

as to the paternity of an oft-repeated joke is
frequently out of the question. What I have
done in these volumes is, by gathering the *mots*
from contemporary lives, diaries, memoirs,
autobiographies *et hoc genus omne*, to get as
near as may be to correctness.

The sayings of Sydney Smith—a wit, like the
Sixty, of the temple, not of the tavern—as will
be seen in the following pages, are of various
kinds, from the lightning flashes of wit, to
wild, rollicking, uproarious humour. As Tom
Moore said of him in his *Diary:* "He never
minds what nonsense he talks, which is one
of the great reasons of his saying so much
that is comical." Another entry in the same
Diary reads: "Sydney at dinner and after
in full force; sometimes high comedy, sometimes farce; both perfect in their way. Sydney
most rampantly facetious." Often the *mot* that
flashed out in conversation was afterwards employed in his writings: as Moncton Milnes (Lord
Houghton) put it: "Smith always exercises
his jokes in society before he runs them upon
paper." Lord Lansdowne excellently described
Sydney Smith as "a mixture of Punch and
Cato." Landor addressed him as "Humour's
pink primate, Sydney Smith." In the *Noctes*,
too, he is described as "a rare genius of the grotesque, with his quips and cranks a formidable
enemy to pomposity and pretension. No man
can wear a big wig comfortably in his presence."

Indeed what Smith's contemporaries have written of his wit would fill as large a volume as the examples of his wit that have come down to us. In the hope that some idea of the man himself as he spoke them, may be more present in reading his *mots*, a few of these thumb-nail notes on Sydney Smith as a wit are here transcribed :—Sydney Smith's conversation was the conversation of a man mad with spirits.—His intellect was like an electric coil, you touched it and it flashed out in sparkling coruscations at the touch. —Possessing as much wit as a man without a grain of his sense, he had as much sense as a man without a spark of his wit.—Macaulay said of him that it seemed to be his greatest luxury to keep his wife and daughters laughing for two or three hours every day.—The lips of Sydney Smith dropping sparkling diamonds of wit every now and then, attention to which was demanded by the speaker's own boisterous laugh.—Crabb Robinson wrote of Smith in his *Diary* that his "faun-like face was a sort of promise of good things when he did but open his lips."—Lord Dudley said to Sydney Smith : "You have been laughing at me for the last seven years, and yet in all that time you never said a single thing to me I wished unsaid."—His talk is a torrent of wit, fun, nonsense, pointed remark, just observation, and happy illustrations.—No stain of impurity ever sullied his blade. —"Sydney," said one of his college chums, "your sense, wit, and clumsiness always give me the idea of an Athenian carter."—His casual *bon-mots* wreathed the town with smiles. —A wise man in the brilliant guise of a wit.—His inevitable and irresistible flood of fun rolled over one like a cataract, never ceasing, never slackening, never varying its pace for an instant. The following is an outline of his life:—1771. Sydney Smith was born on June 3rd at Woodford, Essex; his father was Robert Smith; his mother, Maria Olier, daughter of a French emigrant. —1782. Scholar of Winchester College.—1789. New College, Oxford; fellowship two years later. — 1794. Left College and entered the Church. Curate of Nether Avon, Wilts.—1798. Went to Edinburgh as tutor.— 1800. Married Catherine Pybus.—1802. Started the *Edinburgh Review* in conjunction with Brougham, Jeffrey, Francis Horner and others. —1803. Left Edinburgh for London. Preacher at the Foundling Hospital; lectured on Moral Philosophy at the Royal Institution.—1807. Rector of Foston-le-Clay, Yorkshire, "Village parson and doctor." *Peter Plymley's Letters.* —1828. Canon of Bristol.—1829. Rector of Combe Florey.—1831. Canon Residentiary of St Paul's.—1845. February 22nd, died.

W. J.

RICHARD BRINSLEY SHERIDAN.

"A TRUE-TRAINED wit lays his plan like a general—foresees the circumstances of the conversation—surveys the ground and contingencies—and detaches a question to draw you into the palpable ambuscade of his ready-made joke." So wrote Sheridan, and his practice showed him, according to his own definition, to be a "true-trained wit," for often the *bon-mot* was carefully elaborated and then the conversation as carefully guided to a fitting point at which the wit might be brought forth with apparent spontaneity. This idea of wit is very different from the general one which is wittily defined by Sydney Smith when he called wit "in midwife's phrase, a quick conception and an easy delivery." Each of these wits defined wit as it was exemplified in his own practice; with Smith as with Douglas Jerrold, the joke flashed to the tip of the tongue and must out "though the heavens should crack and the dearest friend take it amiss." With Sheridan it was far otherwise, and one of his biographers has shown the world how carefully he elaborated the thought which was ultimately perfected as used in the House of Commons, when Sheridan said that the previous speaker was indebted to his imagination for his facts and his memory for his wit.

Many of Sheridan's recorded sayings are, however, obviously retorts on the spur of the
moment; and the testimony of several of his
contemporaries is that his wit was at times so
incessant that it could but be spontaneous.—
Mrs Le Fanu, his sister, said that the same
playful fancy, the same sterling and innoxious
wit, that was shown afterwards in his writings, cheered and delighted the family circle.—
" Sheridan's humour, or rather wit," said Lord
Byron, " was always saturnine, and sometimes
savage. He never laughed, at least that I saw,
and I watched him. In society I have met him
frequently ; he was superb."—His wit was an
incessant flame. — He sometimes displayed a
kind of serious and elegant playfulness, not
apparently rising to wit, but unobservedly
saturated with it, which was unspeakably
pleasing.—His wit is the wit of common sense.
—Grace of manner, charm of voice, fluency
of language, and, above all, a brilliancy of
sarcasm, a wit and a humour ; and again a
felicity of statement that made him the delight
of every audience, and that excited the admiration of his very opponents themselves.—The
wit displayed by Sheridan in Parliament was
perhaps, from the suavity of his temper, much
less sharp than brilliant.—The story of his
life told in outline is as follows :—1751. Richard
Brinsley Butler Sheridan was born on October
30th in Dublin ; his father, Thomas Sheridan,

an actor manager ; his mother, Frances
Chamberlaine, an accomplished authoress.—
1762. At school at Harrow, where he remained
for five or six years. — 1773. Married Miss
Linley, a noted beauty and singer.—1775. *The
Rivals ; St Patrick's Day, or the Scheming
Lieutenant*, and the *Duenna* produced.—1776.
Sheridan purchased a share in Drury Lane
Theatre.—1777. *A Trip to Scarborough*, and
The School for Scandal.—1779. *The Critic.*—
1780. Entered Parliament as member for Staf-
ford.—1782. Under-Secretary of State in the
Rockingham Administration.—1783. Secretary
to the Treasury in the Coalition Ministry.—
1787. One of the accusers in the Impeachment
of Warren Hastings.—1788. Made his great
speech in the impeachment. Production of
Pizarro.—1809. Drury Lane Theatre burnt.—
1816. July 7, died.

W. J.

SYDNEY SMITH.

BON-MOTS

OF

SYDNEY SMITH.

A WORTHY baronet who dabbled in politics came to Sydney Smith one day very much irritated.

"What is the matter?" was the immediate question, "are any of our institutions in danger?"

"No, but I have just been with Brougham, whom I sought out for the purpose of making an important communication, but, upon my word, he treated me as if I were a fool."

"Never mind, my dear fellow," said Smith, in his most sympathetic tones, "never mind, never mind, he thought you knew it!"

THE whole of my life (said Smith to a friend), has been passed like a razor—in hot water or a scrape.

—⁓ΛΛΛ⁓—

DESCRIBING a dinner at which he had been present, Sydney Smith said : " Puns are frequently provocative. One day, after dinner with a Nabob, he was giving us Madeira—

" ' *London—East India—picked—particular,*'

then a second thought struck him, and he remembered that he had a few flasks of Constantia in the house, and he produced *one*. He gave us just a glass apiece. We became clamorous for another, but the old qui-hi was firm in his refusal.

" 'Well, well,' said I, ' since we can't double the Cape, we must e'en go back to Madeira.'

" We all laughed, our host most of all, and he, too, luckily had his joke, ' Be of Good Hope, you shall double it,' at which we all laughed still more immoderately, and drank the second flask."

—⁓ΛΛΛ⁓—

IT is admirable of you to send game to the clergy ; *that* is what I call real piety ; it reminds one of the primitive Christians.

TWO well-known men were being discussed. Said Smith: "There is the same difference between their tongues as between the hour and the minute hand; one goes twelve times as fast, and the other signifies twelve times as much."

—◦◦◦—

BLANCO WHITE used to relate that he once complained to Sydney Smith of long and weary nights of utter sleeplessness, owing to bad health. "I can furnish you," replied Smith, "with an infallible soporific. I have published two volumes of Sermons. I will send them to you; they will last a long time. You are to take them into bed with you, and begin at the beginning. Before you have read three pages you will be fast; but take care that you put the candle in a safe place, or you will sleep so sound, you will be burned to death."

—◦◦◦—

TALKING of Milner's *History of Christianity*, Sydney Smith said, "It's a mistake altogether in our friend—no man has a right to write on such subjects, unless he is prepared to go the whole *lamb*."

ON seeing a lady sitting at the dinner-table between two Bishops, Smith enquired, "Her name is Susanna, I assume?"

SOME one having said of Macaulay, "He will let nobody talk but himself," Smith at once answered, "Why, who would if he could help it?"

AT one of Rogers's breakfast-parties Sydney Smith is reported to have said, "I wish I could write poetry like you, Rogers, I would write an *Inferno*, and I would put Macaulay among a lot of disputants—and gag him!"

A YOUNG clergyman tremblingly asked the Canon how he liked his preaching. "Well, if you must know," came the answer, "I like you better in the bottle than in the wood."

OF Horner, one of his early colleagues on the *Edinburgh Review*, Sydney Smith said that he had the Ten Commandments written on his face, and looked so virtuous that he might commit any crime with impunity.

YES, X. was merry, not wise. You know a man of small understanding is merry where he can, not where he should. Lightning must, I should think, be the wit of the heavens.

—∿∧∿—

A LEARNED bore was dwelling at inordinate length upon the great size of a fly's eye compared with its bulk, when Sydney Smith flatly contradicted him, quoting triumphantly, these words from the *Death of Cock Robin*,

> "I, said the fly, with my *little* eye,
> I saw him die."

—∿∧∿—

" I WILL explain it to you," said W. D.
        "Oh, pray don't, my dear fellow," said Sydney, laughing, "I did understand a little about the Scotch Kirk before you undertook to explain it to me yesterday ; but now my mind is like a London fog on the subject."

—∿∧∿—

NO, I don't like dogs ; I always expect them to go mad. A lady asked me once for a motto for her dog Spot. I proposed, "Out, damned Spot," but she did not think it sentimental enough.

TAKING up the cartoon of the Beautiful Gate, Sydney Smith began reading the fine speech of St Peter to the beggar, "Silver and gold have I none."

"Ah! that was in the time of the paper currency," said he.

—⁓⋀⋀⋀⋁⋀⋁⋀⁓—

SYDNEY SMITH said that he had got rid of the two great bores of society, invitation and introduction, and that he literally went to routs without either.

—⁓⋀⋀⋀⋁⋀⁓—

TALKING with Southey over their mutual friends, Sydney Smith referred to Charles Lamb's intemperate habits. "He draws so much beer that no wonder he buffoons people —he must have a *butt* to put it in."

—⁓⋀⋀⋀⋁⋀⁓—

" ROGERS told us," says Crabb Robinson in his Diary, "that Sydney Smith said to his eldest brother, a grave and prosperous gentleman : 'Brother, you and I are exceptions to the laws of nature. You have risen by your gravity, and I have sunk by my levity.'" *

* Dyce says that Rogers ascribed this *mot* to Horne Tooke.

BISHOP WILBERFORCE describes a most interesting three days spent at Eton at Selwyn's farewell sermon. "I preached once, and he once. He is just setting out, and my friend Whitehead with him as chaplain. Syd-  ney Smith says it will make quite a revolution in the dinners of New Zealand : *tête d' Evêque* will be the most *re- cherché* dish, and your man will add that there is *cold clergyman* on the side-table."

It was on the same occasion that Sydney Smith also said to Selwyn, "And as for myself, my Lord, all I can say is, that when your new parishioners *do* eat you, I sincerely hope you may disagree with them."

—◦◦◦—

A YOUNG man of fashion who was trying to uphold the reputation of a well-known nobleman — accused of cheating at play— thought to clinch his argument by exclaiming, "Well, I don't care what they say, I have just left a card upon him."

"Did you *mark* it then?" enquired Sydney Smith, "otherwise he will not take it as an *honour*."

CALLING upon a fellow writer in the *Edinburgh Review*, Sydney Smith found him actually reading a book for the purpose of reviewing it. Having expressed his astonishment in the strongest terms, his friend inquired how he managed when performing the critical office.

"Oh, I never read a book before reviewing it : it prejudices a man so," was Smith's explanation.

—⋙⋘—

MY friend Tait sent his boy over to spend the day with my boy ; they set him on my boy's pony, and the pony ran away with him, "Oh, ho," cried I, "that is what our lively neighbours call *tête-montée.*"

—⋙⋘—

CAMPBELL, the poet, tells how Sydney Smith once said to him that if Hallam were in the midst of a full assembly of scientific men, and if Euclid were to enter the room with his Elements under his arm and were to say, "Gentlemen, I suppose no one present doubts the truth of the Forty-fifth Proposition of my first Book of Elements"—Mr Hallam would immediately say, "Yes, *I* have my doubts."

A SCANDALISED fop pointed out, with a grimace of disgust, a straw on the carpet of a drawing-room filled with people of fashion, thereby implying that some unworthy plebeian had driven to the door in a hackney coach. "God bless my soul," said Sydney Smith, "do you care about that? Why, I was at a *literary soirée* the other night where the carpet was like a stubble field."

—⁓⁓⁓—

SYDNEY SMITH was talking over the subject of American Slavery with his friend Mr Everett, when Everett observed in a tone of tender self-pity, that we in England did not really understand the matter, and could not feel at our distance how impossible it was to associate with the negroes, they smelt so abominably.

"Ah!" retorted Smith, without a moment's hesitation, "'At si non alium late jactasset odorem *civis* erat' ('laurus erat,' in Virgil). That, sir, may be a reason for not inviting him to a crowded evening party, but it is no reason for refusing them their freedom."

—⁓⁓⁓—

OBSERVING Lord Brougham's one-horse carriage, Smith remarked to a friend, alluding to the B surmounted by a coronet on the panel, "There goes a carriage with a B outside and a *wasp* within."

MRS LONGMAN being about to entertain at dinner the two noted entomologists, Kirby and Spence, Sydney Smith suggested a menu which should include "flea-pâtes, earth worms on toast, caterpillars crawling in cream and removing themselves," &c.

TOM MOORE asked Smith to accompany him to Newton's studio to see his (Moore's) portrait. Smith paused for a moment in front

of the picture, then, turning to the painter, said, "Couldn't you contrive to throw into his face somewhat of a stronger expression of hostility to the Church Establishment?"

SYDNEY SMITH, walking with the Bishop of Exeter, saw written up over a shop, "Tongues cured here."
"Shall we go in, my lord?"

SIR RODERICK MURCHISON, according to Sydney Smith, would be found giving "not *swarries*, but *quarries;* all the ladies having ivory-handled hammers and six little bottles for each to try the stones."

—◊◊◊—

MACAULAY had told Sydney Smith that meeting him was some compensation for missing Ramohun Roy. Sydney broke forth: "Compensation! Do you mean to insult me? A beneficed clergyman, an ortho-dox clergyman, a nobleman's chaplain, to be no more than compensation for a Brahmin; and a heretic Brahmin, too, a fellow who has lost his own reli-gion and can't find another; a  vile heterodox dog, who, as I am credibly in-formed eats beef-steaks in private! A man who has lost his caste! who ought to have melted lead poured down his nostrils, if the good old *Vedas* were in force as they ought to be."

—◊◊◊—

ON Mrs Austin explaining that she was no relation to Miss Austen, Sydney Smith said to her, "You are quite wrong; I always let it be inferred that I am the son of Adam Smith."

NOTHING amuses me more than to observe the utter want of perception of a joke in some minds. Mrs Jackson called one day and spoke of the oppressive heat.

"Heat, ma'am!" I said, "it was so dreadful here that I found there was nothing left for it but to take off my flesh and sit in my bones."

"Take off your flesh and sit in your bones, sir! Oh, Mr Smith! how could you do that?" she exclaimed, with the utmost gravity.

"Nothing more easy, ma'am; come and see next time." But she ordered her carriage and evidently thought it a very unorthodox proceeding.

—◊◊◊—

TALKING once of charades and such like literary minutiæ, Smith said that charades if made at all should be made without benefit of clergy; the offender should instantly be hurried off to execution, and be cut off in the middle of his dulness, without being allowed to explain to his executioner why his first is like his second or what is the resemblance between his fourth and his ninth.

—◊◊◊—

IT is a grand thing for a man to find out his own line and keep to it—you get so much further and so much faster on your own rail.

EXPLAINING the scantiness of Scotch scholarship, Sydney Smith said, "Greek was a witch, and, as such, could not cross running water, nor ever get beyond the Tweed."

—⁓⁓⁓—

WAR was being discussed when Sydney Smith said that in some causes he would allow fighting to be a luxury, adding that the business of prudent, sensible men was to guard against luxury. *

—⁓⁓⁓—

SYDNEY SMITH said that he must believe in apostolical succession, there being no other way of accounting for the descent of the (then) Bishop of Exeter from Judas Iscariot.

—⁓⁓⁓—

REFERRING to the fact of men so often colliding with one another over different questions, Smith exclaimed, "How few men are on the right rail!"

—⁓⁓⁓—

THERE is not the least use in preaching to anyone, *unless you chance to catch them ill*.

* He happily used the same idea in a characteristic letter to Lady Grey.

TO some one who had said that Whewell's forte was science,—"Yes, and his foible is omni-science."

—⁓⁓⁓—

DINING at a friend's, Sydney Smith happened to meet Mr B., whom he always met with pleasure, as he was a man of sense, simplicity, and learning, but with such a total absence of humour in himself and of per-ception of it in others as made him an amusing object of speculation to the wit.

The conversation at the table took a liberal turn. Sydney Smith in the full career of his spirits happened to say that though he was not generally considered an illiberal man, yet he must confess he had a little weakness, one secret wish—he would like *to roast a Quaker*.

"Good Heavens, Mr Smith!" said Mr B. full of horror, "roast a Quaker?"

"Yes, sir!" (with the greatest gravity) "roast a Quaker."

"But do you consider, Mr Smith, the torture?"

"Yes, sir," replied Sydney, "I have con-sidered everything. It may be wrong, as you

say ; the Quaker would undoubtedly suffer
acutely, but everyone has his tastes,—mine
would be to roast a Quaker. One would
satisfy me, only one. It is one of those
peculiarities I have striven against in vain,
and I hope you will pardon my weakness."

Mr B.'s honest simplicity could stand this
no longer, and he seemed hardly able to sit at
table with him. The whole company were in
roars of laughter at the scene ; but neither
this, nor the mirth and mischief sparkling in
Sydney's eyes, enlightened him in the least,
for a joke was a thing of which he had no
conception.

At last Smith, seeing that he was giving real
pain, said, " Come, come, Mr B., since you
think I am so very illiberal, I must be wrong,
and will give up my roasted Quaker, rather
than your esteem ; let us drink wine together."

Peace was made, but it is doubtful whether
time or explanation ever made B. comprehend
that it was a joke.

—◦◦◦◦—

SIR ANTHONY PANIZZI (librarian of the
British Museum) was talking to Sydney
Smith at a grand reception when the venerable
Thomas Grenville entered. " Ah ! " exclaimed
Smith to his companion, " here comes the man
from whom we all ought to learn how to grow
old."

" THE great use of the raised centre revolving on a round table," said Sydney Smith, "would be to put Macaulay ('the talk-mill') on it, and so distribute his talk fairly to the company."

—⁓⁓⁓—

MELBOURNE used to begin by damning the subject of conversation. I used to say, " Well, well, suppose it damned, and proceed with the discussion !"

—⁓⁓⁓—

IN conversation once, after listening to some one's anecdotage, Sydney Smith remarked with all solemnity that a certain ancient people ate their old members who became troublesome, and told long stories.

—⁓⁓⁓—

SMITH was very comical about a remedy of Lady Holland's for the book-worms in the library at Holland House, having the books washed with some mercurial preparation. He said it was Sir Humphry Davy's opinion that the air would become charged with the mercury, and that the whole family would be salivated, adding, " I shall see Allen some day, with his tongue hanging out, speechless, and shall take the opportunity to stick a few principles into him."

THE same passion which peoples the parsonage with chubby children, animates the Arminian, and burns in the breast of the Baptist.

—◦◦◦—

MRS B. has not very clear ideas about the tides. I remember at a large party, her insisting that it was always high-tide at London

Bridge at twelve o'clock. She referred to me. " Now, Mr Smith, is it not so?"

I answered, " It used not to be so, I believe, formerly, but perhaps the Lord Mayor and Aldermen have altered it lately."

—◦◦◦—

SIR Henry Holland was so smooth mannered that Sydney Smith once said of him that ' he was all mucilage, he was so very bland."

SYDNEY SMITH talked once of his house being full of cousins, adding that they were all first cousins, and he wished them— once removed.

—∿∿∿—

ON Matthews saying on some occasion of Tom Hill, "Will nobody stop that fellow's mouth?" "Not *me*," said Smith, "I know the way to Highgate but not to muzzle Hill" (Muswell Hill).

—∿∿∿—

SOME people were assembled to look at a turtle that had been sent to the house of a friend, when a child of the party stooped down and began eagerly stroking its shell.

"Why are you doing that?" said Sydney Smith.

"Oh, to please the turtle."

"Why, child, you might as well stroke the dome of St Paul's to please the Dean and Chapter."

—∿∿∿—

DURING one of the famous breakfasts at Samuel Rogers', the talk was of stories of dram-drinkers catching fire: Smith pursued the idea in every possible shape. The inconvenience of a man coming too near the candle when he was speaking, "Sir, your observation has caught fire!" He then went on to imagine a parson breaking into a blaze in the pulpit; the engines called to put him out—no water to be had, the man at the waterworks being an Unitarian or an Atheist.

—ⱲⱲ—

WHILST at Combe Florey, as Smith was writing one day in his favourite bay window, a pompous little gentleman in rusty black was ushered in.

"May I ask what procures me the honour of this visit?" enquired Smith.

"Oh," said the little man, "I am compounding a history of the distinguished families of Somersetshire, and have called to obtain the Smith arms."

"I regret, sir," responded Smith, "not to be able to contribute to so valuable a work; but the Smiths never had any arms, and have invariably sealed their letters with their thumbs."

—ⱲⱲ—

TO one who expressed a very strong opinion, and justified it on the ground that he was only a plain man, Sydney Smith retorted that he was not aware that the gentleman's personal appearance had anything to do with the question.

WHEN Lord Jeffrey was having a cast of his face taken, Sydney Smith, who was present, on seeing the face of his friend completely covered with the plaster, leaped up, exclaiming mock heroically, " There's immortality ! but God keep me from such a mode of obtaining it."

—◌◌◌—

A BEE came in through the open window at a dinner party, when, turning to a lady who sat next to him, a conceited young officer 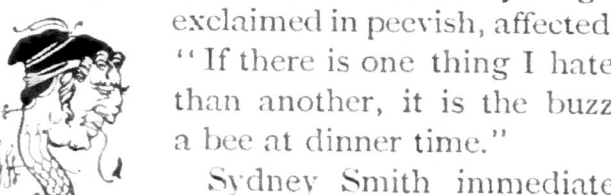 exclaimed in peevish, affected tones, " If there is one thing I hate more than another, it is the buzzing of a bee at dinner time."

Sydney Smith immediately remarked in an undertone to his fair neighbour, " I suppose, madam, if a hornet came in, the captain would *sell out !*"

—◌◌◌—

SOMEONE mentioned a young Scotchman who was about to marry an Irish widow double his age, and of very large (considerable) proportions. " Going to marry her !" Smith exclaimed, bursting out laughing. " Impossible ; you mean a part of her. He could not marry all of her himself. It would not be a case of bigamy, but of trigamy. The neighbourhood or the magistrate should interfere.

There is enough of her to furnish wives for the whole parish. One man marry her! it is monstrous! you might people a colony with her, or, perhaps, take your morning's walk round her, always providing that there were frequent resting-places, and you were in rude health. I once was rash enough to walk round her before breakfast, but only got half-way and gave it up exhausted. Or you might read the Riot Act, and disperse her ; in short you might do anything but marry her."

"Oh," said a young lady present, recovering from the general laugh, "did you make that all up yourself?'"

"Yes, Lucy, all myself, child, all my own thunder. Do you think when I am about to make a joke, I send for my neighbours or consult the clerk and churchwardens upon it?"

" THE miseries of human life," said Sydney Smith, on one occasion, "were things only to be successfully encountered on a basis of beef and wine."

A DEVONSHIRE elector (some time in the thirties) expressed surprise at Lord John Russell's small stature. Sydney Smith explained it by saying it was because Lord John "was wasted in the country's service."

AN American said to Sydney Smith, "You are so funny! Do you know, you remind me of our great joker, Dr Chamberlayne."

"I am much honoured," Smith replied; "but I was not aware that you had such a functionary in the United States."

—◊◊◊—

SIR EDWIN LANDSEER somewhat patronisingly offered to let Sydney Smith sit to him for his portrait.

"Is thy servant a dog," retorted Sydney Smith, "that he should do this thing?"*

—◊◊◊—

I DO not mean to be disrespectful, but the attempt of the Lords to stop the progress of reform reminds me very forcibly of the great storm of Sidmouth, and of the conduct of the excellent Mrs Partington on that occasion. In the winter of 1824 there set in a great flood upon that town—the tide rose to an incredible height—the waves rushed in upon the houses—and everything was threatened with destruction. In the midst of this sublime and horrible storm, Dame Partington, who lived upon the beach,

* This *mot* has always been ascribed to Sydney Smith ; it was so when first current in the thirties, though Lord Houghton in his *Monographs* states that Lockhart really said it.

was seen at the door of her house with mops and pattens, trundling her mop, squeezing out the sea-water, and vigorously pushing away the Atlantic Ocean. The Atlantic was roused. Mrs Partington's spirit was up, but I need not tell you that the contest was unequal. The Atlantic Ocean beat Mrs Partington. She was excellent at a slop or a puddle, but she should not have meddled with a tempest. Gentlemen, be at your ease—be quiet and steady. You will beat Mrs Partington.

—᙮ᗯᐯᗯ᙮—

OF a preacher noted for his dull sermons, Sydney Smith said that he evidently thought that sin was to be taken from men as Eve was from Adam—by casting them into a deep sleep.

—᙮ᗯᐯᗯ᙮—

TO illustrate the wasting of the moments that make up the year, Sydney Smith remarked to a young lady, " Do you ever reflect how you pass your life? If you live to seventy-two, which I hope you may, your life is passed in the following manner :—An hour a day is three years, this makes twenty-seven years sleeping ; nine years dressing ; nine years at table ; six years playing with children ; nine years walking, drawing, and visiting ; six years shopping, and three years quarrelling."

SYDNEY Smith said that he found the influence of the aristocracy "oppressive," but added, "However, I never failed, I think, to speak my mind before any of them ; I hardened myself early."

—wWw—

SYDNEY SMITH had, it is well known, a preference for London sights and sounds to all that the country could offer ; the

tastes of Young, the actor, were somewhat similar, and when the two met at Holland House, and Young had been mono- polising the conversation for some time, Smith turned to him, saying with much fun, " Do you know, Mr Young, I had much rather be listening to you than to the lowing of oxen or the bleating of sheep."

—wWw—

A LADY of title closely questioned Sydney Smith as to his forbears,—who was his grandfather ?

Smith gravely informed her that " he dis- appeared about the time of the Assizes, and— we asked no questions."

A^N attempt to warm St Paul's Cathedral
Sydney Smith described as useless, saying
that one might as well attempt to warm the
county of Middlesex.

—◦◦◦—

S^{YDNEY} SMITH was annoyed one evening
by the familiarity of a young gentleman,
who, though a new acquaintance, was encour-

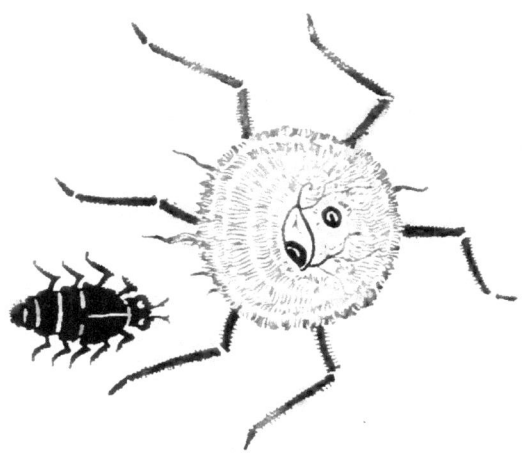

aged by Smith's reputation as a "joker" to
address him by his surname alone. After
awhile the free and easy young man happened
to mention that he was going that evening, for
the first time, to the Archbishop of Canterbury's
palace, and Smith pathetically remarked—

"Let me give you a little bit of advice; pray,
don't clap the Archbishop on the back, and call
him Howley."

ASKED one day at the Kinglakes if he were in favour of increasing the number of the bishops, Smith answered in his vein of humourous exaggeration, "Yes, I *am* for increasing the number of the bishops—those islets in the Bristol Channel, the Flat Holm and the Steep Holm, each should have a bishop."

—ᴧᴧᴧᴧ—

MACAULAY says that he advised Sydney Smith once to stay in London over the meeting of Parliament, and see something of his friends who would be crowding to London. "My flock!" said Smith, "my dear sir, remember my flock! 'The hungry sheep look up and are not fed.'"

—ᴧᴧᴧᴧ—

LORD Dudley was one of the most absent-minded men I think I ever met in society. One day he met me in the street and invited me to meet myself. "Dine with me to-day; dine with me, and I will get Sydney Smith to meet you." I admitted the temptation he held out to me, but said I was engaged to meet him elsewhere.

—ᴧᴧᴧᴧ—

IN Sydney's Smith's last illness, a friend visiting him said that he feared he was very ill, "Yes," was the reply, "not enough of me left to make a curate."

WHAT a beautiful thought — a sunbeam passes through pollution unpolluted.

—∿∿∿—

NEVER give way to melancholy ; resist it steadily, for the habit will encroach. I once gave a lady two and twenty recipes against melancholy ; one was a bright fire ; another to remember all the pleasant things said to and of her ; another to keep a box of sugar-plums on the chimney-piece, and a kettle simmering on the hob. I thought this mere trifling at the moment, but have in after life discovered how true it is that these little pleasures often banish melancholy better than higher or more exalted objects ; that no means ought to be thought too trifling which can oppose it either in ourselves or others.

—∿∿∿—

LIFE is a difficult thing in the country, I assure you ; and it requires a good deal of forethought to steer the ship when you live twelve miles from a lemon. By-the-bye, that reminds me of one of our greatest domestic triumphs. Some years ago my friend C—, the arch-epicure of the Northern Circuit, was dining with me. On sitting down to dinner, he turned round to the servant and desired him to look in his greatcoat pocket, and he would find a lemon ; "for," he said, "I thought it likely you might have duck and green peas for dinner, and therefore thought it prudent at this distance from a town to provide a lemon."

I turned round and exclaimed indignantly,— "Bunch, bring in the lemon bag," and Bunch appeared with a bag containing a dozen lemons. He respected us wonderfully after that. Oh ! it is reported that he goes to bed with concentrated lozenges of wild-duck, so as to have the taste constantly in his mouth when he awakes in the night.

—◦◦◦—

YES, I have the greatest possible respect for him ; but from his feeble voice, he always reminds me of a liberal blue-bottle fly. He gets his head down and his hand on your button, and pours into you an uninterrupted stream of whiggism in a low buzz. I have known him intimately, and conversed constantly with him for the last thirty years, and give him credit for the most enlightened mind, and a genuine love of public virtue ; but I can safely say that during that period, I have never heard one single syllable he has uttered.

SOMEONE having mentioned a certain marriage as about to take place, Smith said that it would be like the union of an acid and an alkali ; the result must be a *tertium quid*, or neutral salt.

MONCTON MILNES had been talking to an Alderman, when the latter turned away. Smith said to Milnes, " You were speaking to the Lord Mayor elect. I myself felt in his presence like the Roman whom Pyrrhus tried to frighten with an elephant and who— remained calm."

OTHER rules vary : this is the only one you will find without exception—that, in this world, the salary or reward is always in the inverse ratio of the duties performed.

SOMEONE spoke of the financial embarrassment of University College at that time. " Yes, it is so great that I understand they have already seized on the air-pump, the exhausted receiver, and galvanic batteries ; and that bailiffs have been seen chasing the Professor of Modern History around the quadrangle."

IN talking of the Irish Church and pronounc-
ing it a nuisance, Sydney Smith said, "I
have always compared it to setting up butcher's
shops in Hindostan, where they don't eat meat.
'We don't want this,' they say. 'Aye, aye,
true enough, but you must *support our shop.*'"

—∿∿∿—

OH! don't read those twelve volumes till
they are made into a *consommé* of two.
Lord Dudley did still better, he waited till they
blew over.

—∿∿∿—

A JOKE goes a long way in the country. I
have known one last pretty well for seven
years. I remember making a joke, after a
meeting of the clergy in Yorkshire, where there
was a Reverend Mr Buckle who never spoke,
when I gave his health saying that he was a
buckle without a tongue. Most persons within
hearing laughed, but my next neighbour sat
unmoved and sunk in thought. At last, a
quarter of an hour after we had all done, he
suddenly nudged me, exclaiming—

"I see *now* what you meant, Mr Smith;
you meant a joke."

"Yes, sir," I said, "I believe I did," upon
which he began laughing so heartily that I
thought he would choke and was obliged to
pat him on the back.

NEVER neglect your fireplace : I have paid great attention to mine, and could burn you all out in a moment. Much of the cheerfulness of life depends upon it. Who could be miserable with that fire ? What makes a fire so pleasant is, I think, that it is a live thing in a dead room.

—᙮ᐧ᙭᙭ᐧ—

SYDNEY SMITH was sitting at breakfast one morning in the library at Combe Florey, when a poor woman came begging him to christen a new-born infant without loss of time, as she thought it was dying. He instantly quitted the breakfast table for this purpose, and went off to her cottage. On his return, his family enquired in what state he had  left the poor babe. "Why," said he, " I just gave it a dose of castor-oil, and then I christened it ; so now the poor child is ready for either world."

—᙭᙭᙭—

TO take Macaulay out of literature and society, and put him in the House of Commons, is like taking the chief physician out of London during a pestilence.

HARROGATE seemed to me to be the most heaven-forgotten country under the sun. When I saw it there were only nine mangy fir-trees there—and even they all leant away from it.

YES, he has spent all his life in letting down empty buckets into empty wells, and he is frittering away his age in trying to draw them up again.

IT is a great proof of shyness to crumble your bread at dinner. I do it when I sit by the Bishop of London, and with both hands when I sit by the Archbishop.

WHEN so showy a woman as Mrs S. appears anywhere, though there is no garrison within twelve miles, the horizon is immediately clouded with majors.

SOMEONE naming a friend as not very orthodox, Smith said that if you accuse a man of being a Socinian it is all over with him ; for the country gentlemen all think it has something to do with poaching.

ROGERS having praised the gentleness of Smith's horse, "Yes," said Smith, "it is a cross of the rocking horse."

—◦◦◦—

MARRIAGE resembles a pair of shears, so joined that they cannot be separated; often moving in opposite directions, yet always punishing anyone who comes between them.

—◦◦◦—

ONE evening at Sydney Smith's house, a few friends had come in to tea, amongst others Lord Jeffrey and Doctor Holland. Some one spoke of Talleyrand.

"Oh," said Sydney, "Lady Holland laboured incessantly to convince me that Talleyrand was agreeable, and was very angry because his arrival was usually a signal for my departure; but, in the first place, he never spoke at all till he had not only devoured, but digested his dinner, and as this was a slow process with him, it did not occur till everybody else was asleep, or ought to have been so; and when he did speak he was so inarticulate I could never understand a word he said."

"It was otherwise with me," said Doctor Holland, "I never found much difficulty in following him."

" Did not you ? why it was an abuse of terms
to call it talking at all ; for he had no teeth,
and, I believe no roof to his mouth—no uvula
—no larynx—no trachea—no epiglottis—no
anything.   It was not talking, it was gargling ;
and that by-the-bye, now I think of it, must be
the very reason why Holland understood him
so much better than I did."

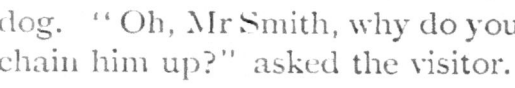

A LADY visitor was walking with Sydney
Smith round the grounds at Combe Florey,
when they came across a fine Newfoundland
dog.   "Oh, Mr Smith, why do you
 chain him up?" asked the visitor.
"Because he has a passion for
breakfasting on parish boys."
"Does he really eat boys, Mr
Smith?"
"Yes, he devours them, buttons and all."
The look of horror on his young friend's face,
said Sydney afterwards, nearly made him die
of laughing.

I LIKE pictures, without knowing anything
about them ; but I hate coxcombry in the
fine arts, as well as in anything else.   I got into
dreadful disgrace with Sir George Beaumont
once, who, standing before a picture at Bowood,
exclaimed, turning to me—

"Immense breadth of light and shade!"
I innocently said, "Yes, about an inch and
a half." He gave me a look that ought to have
killed me.

—⁓∿∿⁓—

CONVERSING in the evening with a small
    circle round Miss Berry's* tea-table Sydney
Smith observed the entrance of a no less
remarkable person both for
talents and for years, dressed
in a beautiful crimson velvet
gown. He started up to meet
his fine old friend, exclaiming, "Exactly the colour of
my preaching cushion," and
leading her forward to the
light he pretended to be lost
in admiration, saying, "I
really can hardly keep my
hands off you; I shall be preaching on you I
fear," and thus he continued in the same playful strain to the infinite amusement of his old
friend and the little circle assembled round her.

—⁓∿∿⁓—

PALMERSTON'S manner of speaking is
    like a man washing his hands;—the
Scotch members don't know what he is doing.

* Miss Berry had been a friend of Doctor Johnson's.

DANIEL WEBSTER struck me as being much like a steam-engine in trousers.

—∿∿∿—

ON one occasion Sydney Smith startled his company with a conundrum, "Why is a horse in good condition like a greyhound in bad?—Because they neither turn a *hare.*"

—∿∿∿—

"I WISH," said Smith once, after listening for some time to his conversational rival, "that Macaulay would see the difference between colloquy and soliloquy."

—∿∿∿—

MACCULLOCH having stated that burials were no test of the number of deaths, "What," said Sydney, "do you mean that people keep private burying-grounds, like skittle-grounds?"

—∿∿∿—

ROGERS having asked Sydney Smith what attitude he recommended him to be taken in, was told, "There is a very expressive one we of the clergy use in first getting up into the pulpit, which might suit you very well" (covering his face with his hands).

A FRIEND commenced saying, " I think I may assert without fear of contradiction—" " Stop, sir," said Smith, " are you acquainted with Mr Hallam ? "

SYDNEY SMITH, at a dinner party, said to his next neighbour, " Now, I know not a soul here present, except you and our host ; so, if I by chance insult or dishonour any of their brothers, sisters, aunts, uncles, or cousins, I take you to witness it is unintentional."

THERE are many people who run about after happiness like an absent-minded man hunting for his hat, which all the while is on his head.

A FINE ideal statue of Satan by Mr Lough failed to find a purchaser, so Sydney Smith suggested that it should be presented to the Reform Club, because " the devil was the first Reformer, and came to grief in Heaven for the too great zeal, indiscretion, and un- timeliness with which he agitated the Reform question ! "

SYDNEY SMITH would often illustrate the weaknesses or foibles of his friends in a telling manner. He said once that Rogers had been in a very bad humour at a dinner party, for Luttrell had been helped to bread sauce before him.

—◦◦◦—

OH ! the observances of the Church concerning feasts and fasts are tolerably well kept, upon the whole, since the rich keep the feasts and the poor the fasts.

—◦◦◦—

ON one occasion a man on the Foston Rectory farm blundered to such an extent that Sydney Smith quite lost his temper, and called him a fool.

"God never made a fool," growled the transgressor.

"That is quite true, sir," was the immediate retort, "but man was not long in making a fool of himself."

—◦◦◦—

CROKER, according to Sydney Smith, would be found at a future moment disputing with the recording angel as to the date of his sins.

WILLIAM CHAMBERS, in conversation
with Sydney Smith, claimed for the
Scotch that they had after all a considerable
fund of humour.   "Oh, by all means—you

are an immensely funny people, but you need
a little operating upon to let the fun out.   I
know no instrument so effectual for the purpose as the *corkscrew!*"

—⟋⋁⋀⋁⋀⟍—

WHAT a talker that Frenchman Buchon
is!—Macaulay is a Trappist compared
to him.

—⟋⋁⋀⋁⋀⟍—

OH! don't mind the caprices of fashionable
women,—they are as gross as poodles fed
on milk and muffins.

WHEN I was going to Brougham Hall, two raw Scotch girls got into the coach in the dark, near Carlisle. " It is very disagreeable getting into a coach in the dark," exclaimed one, after arranging her bandboxes; "one cannot see one's company."

" Very true, ma'am ; and you have a great loss in not seeing me, for I am a remarkably handsome man."

" No, sir ! are you really ? " said both.

" Yes, and in the flower of my youth."

" What a pity," said they.

We soon passed near a lamp-post : they both darted forward to get a look at me.

" La, sir, you seem very stout."

" Oh no, not at all, ma'am; it 's only my greatcoat."

" Where are you going, sir ? "

"To Brougham Hall."

" Why, you must be a very remarkable man to be going to Brougham Hall."

" I am a very remarkable man, ma'am."

At Penrith they got out after having talked incessantly, and tried every possible means to discover who I was, exclaiming as they went off laughing, " Well, it 's very provoking we can't see you; but we 'll find out who you are at the ball. Lord Brougham always comes to the ball at Penrith, and we shall certainly be there, and shall soon discover your name."

SYDNEY SMITH had proposed that Government should pay the Irish Catholic priests.

"They would not take it," said Doctor Doyle.

"Do you mean to say that if every priest in Ireland received to-morrow morning a government letter with a hundred pounds, first quarter of their year's income, that they would refuse it."

"Ah, Mr Smith," said Doctor Doyle, "you've such a way of putting things."

WE find Sydney Smith uttering a wish to capture a Pennsylvanian, apportion his raiment, and give his coat to the widow, his waistcoat to the fatherless, and his breeches to the poor and them that had none to help them. For the witty Canon was a Pennsylvanian bond-holder, and the State had repudiated.

THERE I am, sir, the priest of the Flowery Valley,* in a delightful parsonage, about which I care a good deal, and a delightful country about which I do not care a straw.

I THINK breakfast so pleasant because no one is conceited before one o'clock.

* Combe Florey.

DESCRIBING a visit to Mahomet's Baths at Brighton, where he had been shampooed, Sydney Smith said that they squeezed enough out of him to make a lean curate.

—⁓⋀⋁⋀⁓—

ONE day Rogers took Tom Moore and Sydney Smith home in his carriage from a breakfast; and insisted on showing them, by the way, Dryden's house in some obscure street. It was very wet; the house looked very much like other old houses; and having thin shoes on, they both remonstrated, but in vain. Rogers got out and stood expecting them.

"Oh! you see why Rogers don't mind getting out," said Smith to Moore, laughing and leaning out of the carriage, "he has got goloshes on; but, Rogers, lend us each a golosh and we will then stand on one leg and admire as long as you please."

—⁓⋀⋁⋀⁓—

WHY don't the thieves dress with aprons— so convenient for storing any stolen goods? You would see the Archbishop of York taken off at every race-course, and not a prize-fight without an archdeacon in the paws of the police.

A YOUNG lady said, "Oh, Mr Smith, I cannot bring this flower to perfection."

"Then let me lead," said he gallantly, taking her hand, "perfection to the flower."

—∿∿∿—

BENEVOLENCE is a natural instinct of the human mind.—When A sees B in grievous distress, his conscience always urges him to entreat C to help him.

—∿∿∿—

THE conversation at one of Roger's breakfasts turned upon the American treatment of unpopular persons. "My dear Rogers," said Smith, "if we were both in America, we should be tarred and feathered; and, lovely as we are by nature, I should be an ostrich, and you an emu."

—∿∿∿—

ON an old lady friend being mentioned, Smith said that she was perfection, and always reminded him of an aged angel.

—∿∿∿—

WHEN I praised the author of the New Poor Law the other day, three gentlemen at table took it to themselves and blushed up to the eyes.

I N Sydney Smith's last illness, we are told that the nurse who attended him confessed to having given him a bottle of ink instead of a bottle of physic. He quietly asked her to bring him all the blotting-paper there was in the house.

S OMEONE having said that it was foolish in General Fitzpatrick to insist upon going up alone in the balloon, when it was found that there was not force enough to carry up two, Sydney Smith replied that it was not foolish in General Fitzpatrick, for there is always something sublime in sacrificing to great principles —his profession was courage.

T RUE, it is most painful, not to meet the kindness and affection you feel you have deserved ; but it is a mistake to complain of it —you cannot extort friendship with a cocked pistol.

A FRIEND meeting Sydney Smith enquired after Rogers.

" He is not very well."

" Why, what is the matter ? "

" Oh, don't you know, he has produced a

couplet? When our friend is delivered of a couplet, with infinite labour and pains, he takes to his bed, has straw laid down, the knocker tied up, and expects his friends to call and make enquiries, and the answer at the door invariably is 'Mr Rogers and his little couplet are as well as can be expected.' When he produces an Alexandrine he keeps his bed a day longer."

—∿∧∧∿—

SYDNEY SMITH furnished his house once with a set of daubs, and invented names of great masters for them,—
"a beautiful landscape by Nicholas de Falda, a pupil of Valdeggio, the only painting by that eminent artist!"
He consulted two R.A.s as to his purchases, and when he had set them considering what opportunities were likely to occur, added,

by way of after-thought, "Oh, I ought to have told you, though, that my outside price for a picture is thirty-five shillings!"

—∿∧∧∿—

I AM not fond of expecting catastrophes, but there are *cracks* in the world.

L ORD JOHN RUSSELL said that Sydney
Smith told him that at one time he had
an intention of writing a book of maxims, but
never got beyond the first, which was this :
Generally towards the age of forty, women
got tired of being virtuous, and men of being
honest.

H AVING seen in the newspapers that Sir
Æneas Mackintosh was come to town,
Smith drew such a ludicrous caricature of Sir
Æneas and Lady Dido, for the amusement of
their namesake, that Sir James Mackintosh
rolled on the floor in fits of laughter, and
Sydney Smith, striding across him, exclaimed,
" *Ruat Justitia !* "

" I CALLED on John Taylor," says Crabb
Robinson in his *Diary.* " He is the
eldest of the Norwich family. One of our best
men in all respects. It was of this family that
Sydney Smith said, they reversed the ordinary
saying, that it takes nine tailors to make a
man."

O NE evening when Sydney Smith and Tom
Moore were returning from a dinner-party
at the Longmans', the road being rather

awkward, the coachman was desired to wait at the bottom. "It would never do," said Smith to Moore, "when your *Memoirs* come to be written, to have it said ' He went out to dinner at the house of his respectable publishers, Longmans & Co., and being overturned on his way back was crushed to death by *a large clergyman.*'"

—-ᴡᴡ-—

SAMUEL ROGERS used sometimes at his dinner parties to have candles placed high up all round the dining room to show off the pictures. On his asking Sydney Smith what he thought of the plan, Smith said that he didn't like it at all,—above there was a blaze of light, and below nothing but darkness and gnashing of teeth.

—ᴧᴧᴧ-—

SYDNEY SMITH characterised a good, unworldly, yet witty young curate, as a "happy union of Dean Swift and Parson Adams."

—ᴧᴧᴧ-—

WHAT I have said ought to be done, generally *has* been done ; not, of course, because I have said it, but because it was no longer possible to avoid doing it.

DUELS were under discussion, and Sydney Smith caused much amusement by suggesting that the weapons should be suited to the professions of the combatants. "Imagine, for instance two doctors engaged in a duel with oil of croton on the tips of their fingers."

ONE evening when Sydney Smith was taking tea with Mrs Austin, the servant entered the crowded room with a tea-kettle in his hand, and it seemed doubtful how he could make his way among the numerous groups ; but on the first approach of the steaming kettle, the crowd receded on all sides, Smith among the rest, though carefully watching the progress of the lad to the table.—"I declare," he said, turning to Mrs Austin, "a man who wishes to make his way in life, could do nothing better than go through the world with a boiling tea-kettle in his hand."

I HAVE divided mankind into classes. There is the *Noodle*,—very numerous, but well-known. The *Affliction-woman*,—a valuable member of society, generally an ancient spinster, or distant relation of the family, in small circumstances ; the moment she hears of any

accident or distress in the family, she sets off,
packs up her little bag, and is immediately
established there, to comfort, flatter, fetch and
carry. The *Up-takers*,—a class of people who
only see through their fingers' ends, and go
through a room taking up and touching everything, however visible and however tender.
The *Clearers*,—who begin at the dish before
them, and go on picking or tasting till it is
cleared, however large the company, small the
supply, and rare the contents. The *Sheep-
walkers*,—those who never deviate from the
beaten track, who think as their fathers have
thought since the Flood, who start from a new
idea as they would from guilt. The *Lemon-
squeezers* of society,—people who act on you as
a wet blanket, who see a cloud in the sunshine,
the nails of the coffin in the ribbons of the bride,
predictors of evil, extinguishers of hope ; who,
where there are two sides, see only the worst,—
people whose very look curdles the milk, and
sets your teeth on edge. The *Let-well-aloners*,
—cousins-germane to the *Noodle*, yet a variety ;
people who have begun to think and to act, but
are timid, and afraid to try their wings, and
tremble at the sound of their own footsteps as
they advance, and think it safer to stand still.
Then the *Washerwomen*,—very numerous, who
exclaim, " Well ! as sure as ever I put on my
best bonnet, it is certain to rain," &c. There
are many more, but I forget them.

DINING one day at Mrs Kinglake's (the mother of the historian), Sydney Smith was asked if he would behave as a neighbouring clergyman had done, and refuse to bury a Dissenter.

"On the contrary," he replied, "I should be only too glad to bury them all."

HAVING been asked to give an account of the books he had been reading, Sydney Smith said, "I cannot tell you a thing about them — neither can I catalogue the legs of mutton that I have eaten, and which have made me the man I am."

OF Macaulay, Sydney Smith once said, "Oh yes, we *both* talk a great deal; but I don't believe Macaulay ever did hear my voice. Sometimes when I have told a good story, I have thought to myself :—Poor Macaulay ! he will be very sorry some day to have missed hearing that."

WHEN his physician advised him to "take a walk upon an empty stomach," Smith quietly asked, "Whose?"

THE charm of London is that you are never glad or sorry for ten minutes together; in the country you are the one and the other for weeks.

—~\/\/\/~—

AH! what female heart can withstand a red-coat? I think this should be a part of female education; it is much neglected. As you have the rocking-horse to accustom them to ride, I would have military dolls in the nursery, to harden their hearts against officers and red-coats. I found myself in company with some officers at the country house of a friend once; and as the repast advanced the colonel became very eloquent, and communicated to us a military definition of vice and virtue. "Vice," he said, "was a d—d cocked-tailed fellow; and virtue (striking the table with his fist to enforce the description), was a fellow fenced about for the good of the service." We all burst into such an uncontrollable paroxysm of laughter, that I began to fear the honest colonel might think it for the good of the service to shoot us through the head ; so, for the good of the Church, hastened to agree with him, and we parted very good friends.

—◠◠◠◠—

CALLING one day to inquire after the health of Dr Blake of Taunton, a Radical and a Unitarian, Smith was greeted with the statement, "I am far from well. Though I sit close by a good fire I cannot keep myself warm."

"I can cure you, doctor," said his visitor, as he prepared to go ; "cover yourself with the Thirty-Nine Articles, and you will soon have a delicious glow all over you."

—◠◠◠◠—

SIMPLICITY is a great object in a great book ; it is not wanted in a short one.

—◠◠◠◠—

ON Sydney Smith once saying, in company, that he was formerly very shy, some one asked, "Were you indeed, Mr Smith ? How did you cure yourself?"

"Why, it was not very long before I made two very useful discoveries : first, that all mankind were not solely employed in observing me (a belief that all young people have) ; and next, that shamming was of no use ; that the world was very clear-sighted, and soon estimated a man at his just value. This cured me ; and I determined to be natural, and let the world find me out."

—√√√√—

THE system of tithes ! It is an atrocious way of paying the clergy. The custom of tithe in kind will seem incredible to our posterity ; no one will believe in the ramiferous priest officiating in the corn field.

—√√√√—

YOU will generally see in human life, the round men and the angular men planted in the wrong hole ; but the Bishop of ——, being a round man, has fallen into a triangular hole, and is far better off than many triangular men who have fallen into round holes.

—√√√√—

OF a certain writer Smith said that he made all the country smell like Piccadilly.

—√√√√—

I ONCE saw a dressed statue of Venus in a serious house—the *Venus Millinaria*.

OF course if I ever do go to a fancy dress
ball I should go as a Dissenter.

—⌒∧∧∧⌒—

I ALWAYS tell Lady P. that she has preserved the two impossible concomitants of
a London life—a good complexion and a good
heart.   Most London dinners evaporate in
whispers to one's next door neighbour.   I make
it a rule never to speak a word to mine, but
fire across the table ; though I broke it once
when I heard a lady who sat next me, in a low,

sweet voice, say " No gravy."   I had never
seen her before, but I turned suddenly round
and said, " Madam, I have been looking for
a person who disliked gravy all my life ; let us
swear eternal friendship."   She looked astonished, but took the oath, and what is better,
kept it.   You laugh—but what more usual
foundation for friendship, let me ask, than
similarity of taste ?

S PEAKING of a Revolutionist, Sydney Smith
said that no man could effect great bene-
fits for his country without some sacrifice of the
minor virtues.

—∿∿∿—

O N being overtalked by Macaulay, Sydney
Smith avenged himself with the pleasantry
that Macaulay not only overflowed with learning, but stood in the slops.

—∿∿∿—

I N a discussion upon the ever-green Irish
question, Sydney Smith said that the object
of all government was roast meat, potatoes,
claret, a stout constable, an honest justice, a
clean highway, a free chapel ; that it was
rubbish to be bawling in the streets about the
Emerald Isle, and the Isle of the ocean. The
bold anthem of *Erin go bragh!* A far better
one would be *Erin go bread and cheese; Erin
go cabins that keep out the rain; Erin go
pantaloons without holes in them*, &c.

—∿∿∿—

J EFFREY having been appointed Dean of
the Faculty of Advocates, Sydney Smith
startled a lady from beyond the Tweed with
the alarming announcement that in England
our Deans have no faculties.

YES, he came once to see us in Yorkshire ;
and he was so small and so active, that he
looked exactly like a little spirit running about
in a kind of undress without a body.

—◦◦◦—

" IN a wet summer," said Sydney Smith, " I
had been using the anti-liquid prayer, so
Allen put up a barometer in the vestry, and
remained there during the rest of the service to
watch the effects ; but, I am sorry to say, did
not find them very satisfactory."

—◦◦◦—

THIS is the only sensible Spring I ever remember—a perfect *March* of intellect.

—◦◦◦—

SMITH objected to the superiority of a city
feast, saying to a friend, " I cannot wholly
value a dinner by the *test you do.*"

—◦◦◦—

TO his friends Mrs Tighe and Mrs Cuffe, on
their calling upon him, Smith paid a pretty
compliment, " Ah ! there you are : a *cuff* that
everyone would wear, the *tie* that none would
loose."

IF you masthead a sailor for not doing his duty, why should you not weathercock a parishioner for refusing to pay tithes?

—∿∿∿—

TOM MOORE was enlarging upon a pet theory of his that women could bear pain better than men because of their having less physical sensibility. This was unanimously exclaimed against. He offered to put it to the test by bringing in a hot tea-pot, which he would answer for the ladies of the party being able to hold for a much longer time than the men. Sydney Smith at once began comically enlarging upon Moore's cruelty to the female part of the creation, and the practice he must have had in such experiments. " He has been all his life," said Smith, " trying the sex with hot tea-pots; the burning ploughshare was nothing to it. I think I hear his terrific tone in a *tête-à-tête*—' Bring a tea-pot!'"

A FEW yards in London dissolve or cement friendship.

—·v\/\/v—

SYDNEY SMITH had not much sympathy with the increase of colonial bishops—or "colonial mitrophilism" as he termed it—saying that soon there would not be a rock in the sea on which a cormorant can perch, but they would put a bishop beside it.

—·v\/\/v—

A FRIEND complaining of the interminable length of speeches in the House of Commons, Sydney Smith said, "Don't talk to me of not being able to cough a speaker down —just try the whooping cough!"

—·v\/\/v—

"MACAULAY is improved! Macaulay improves!" exclaimed Sydney Smith of his great rival talker, "I have observed in him of late—brilliant flashes of silence!"

—·v\/\/v—

IF you are every day thinking whether you have done anything for the *Flowers of History*, of course you will be unhappy.

AT one of Rogers' "breakfasts" at which Hallam was present, Jeffrey arrived late. "Ah!" exclaimed Sydney Smith, greeting him, "we know you have been detained trying the case of Hallam *v.* Everybody."

I *CANNOT* cure myself of punctuality.

MRS MARCET having complained of sleeplessness, Sydney Smith said, "I can furnish you with a perfect soporific. I have published two volumes of sermons, take them to bed with you. I recommended them once to Blanco White, and, before the third page, he was fast."

AT a meeting in which Sydney Smith spoke eloquently in favour of Catholic Emancipation in 1825, a poor clergyman whispered to him that he was quite of his way of thinking, —but had nine children.

"I begged he would remain a Protestant," added Smith, in telling the story.

THERE is no limit to Macaulay's knowledge, on small subjects as well as great—he is like a book in breeches.

DURING a dinner at Spencer House, the conversation, turning upon dogs, brought out a curious revelation.

"Oh!" said Sydney Smith, "one of the greatest difficulties I have had with my parishioners has been on the subject of dogs."

"How so?" enquired Lord Spencer.

"Why, when I first went down into Yorkshire,

there had not been a resident clergyman in my parish for a hundred and fifty years. Each farmer kept a huge mastiff dog, ranging a large, and ready to make his morning meal on clergy or laity as best suited his particula taste; I never could approach a cottage in pursuit of my calling, but I rushed into the jaws of one of these shaggy monsters. scolded, preached, and prayed without avail so I determind to try what fears for their pockets might do. Forthwith appeared in the county papers a minute account of a trial of a farmer at the Northampton Sessions for keeping dogs unconfined ; where said farmer was not only fined five pounds, and reprimanded by the magistrates, but sentenced to three months' imprisonment. The effect was wonderful, and the reign of Cerberus ceased in the land."

"That accounts," said Lord Spencer, "for what has puzzled me and Althorp for many years. We never failed to attend the Sessions at Northampton, and we could never find out how we had missed this remarkable dog case."

—~∧∧∧∧~—

SYDNEY SMITH asked a friend how herrings should be *dressed*—or should they be eaten *naked ?*

—~∧∧∧∧~—

SOMEONE asked if a certain bishop was not about to marry. "Perhaps he may,' said Sydney, "Yet how can a bishop marry ? How can he flirt? The most he can say is—' I will see you in the vestry after service.'

—~∧∧∧∧~—

THE Puseyite priest with his little volume of nonsense.

HAVE you heard of Niebuhr's discoveries? All Roman history reversed. Tarquin turning out an excellent family man, and Lucretia a very doubtful character whom Lady Davy would not have visited.

MEN of small incomes, be it known, have often very acute feelings; and a curate trod on feels a pang as great as when a bishop is refuted.

SYDNEY SMITH, when preaching in Edinburgh, seeing how almost exclusively congregations were made up of ladies, took for his text the verse from the Psalms, "Oh, that *men* would therefore praise the Lord!" with facetious emphasis laid upon the word *men*.

I WILL do human nature the justice to say that we are all prone to make *other* people do their duty.

MR P—— said: "I always write best with an amanuensis."

"Oh! but are you quite sure that he puts down what you dictate, my dear P——?

A T a dinner where H. Reeve was expected, the host said, "We are so sorry poor Reeve is laid up with the gout."

"Reeve with the gout?" echoed Smith, "I should have thought rheumatism was good enough for him."

—·∧∧∧·—

O N one occasion, a gentleman in the coach with me, with whom I had been conversing for some time, suddenly looked out of the window as we approached York, and said—

"There is a very clever man, they say, but a damned odd fellow, lives near here—Sydney Smith, I believe."

"He may be a very odd fellow," said I, taking off my hat to him and laughing, "and I dare say he is; but odd as he is, he is here, very much at your service." Poor man! I thought he would have sunk into his boots, and vanished through the bed of the carriage, he was so distressed; but I thought I had better tell him at once, or he might proceed to say I had murdered my grandmother, which I must have resented, you know.

DEAN C——? Oh! his only adequate punishment would be to be preached to death by wild curates.

—∿∿∿—

MEETING a friend who had grown much stouter, Smith greeted him with, "Why, I didn't half see you when we met last year."

—∿∿∿—

HAS W. increased his library? Yes, it has overflowed all the lower rooms, and has crawled up the staircase, and covers the walls like an erysipelas.

—∿∿∿—

SAID Smith of some one:—He has no command over his understanding; it is always getting between his legs and tripping him up.

—∿∿∿—

LANDSEER said that with Sydney Smith's love of humour it must be a great act of self-denial to abstain from going to the theatres. To this Smith replied that the managers were very polite; they sent him free admissions which he *could* not use, and he in return sent them free admissions to St Paul's, which they *did* not use.

" ON my remarking," says Moore, "how well and good-humouredly our host had mixed us all up together, Smith said, 'That's the great use of a good conversational cook, who says to his company, "I'll make a good pudding of you"; it's no matter what you came into the bowl, you must come out a pudding. "Dear me," says one of the ingredients, "wasn't I just now an egg?" but he feels the batter sticking to him,'" &c., &c.

—⁓∿⁓—

SYDNEY SMITH once told a visitor to his Yorkshire parsonage that the hams at his table were the only genuine hams—other people's were mere Shems and Japhets.

—⁓∿⁓—

ON Mrs Grote, gorgeous with a rose-coloured turban, entering a drawing-room, Smith said suddenly to his companion, "Now I know the meaning of the word grotesque."

—⁓∿⁓—

WHEN Sydney Smith lost a few hundreds by the Pennsylvania Bonds, a publisher called on him offering to retrieve his fortunes, if he would get up a three-volume novel.

"Well, sir," said Smith, after some seeming

consideration, "if I do so, I can't travel out of my own line, *ne sutor ultra crepidam*. I must have an archdeacon for my hero, to fall in love with the pew-opener, with the clerk for a confidant — tyrannical interference of the churchwardens — clandestine correspondence concealed under the hassocks—appeal to the parishioners, &c."

"All that, sir," said the publisher, "I would not presume to interfere with ; I would leave it entirely to your own inventive genius."

"Well, sir, I am not prepared to come to terms at present, but if ever I do undertake such a work, you shall certainly have the refusal."

—— -ᴧ/\/\ᴧ——

ENUMERATING and acting the different sorts of hand-shaking to be met with in society, Smith said there were : the *digitory*, or one finger, exemplified in Lord Brougham, who puts forth his forefinger, and says with his strong northern accent, "How *arrre* you?" The *sepulchral* or *mortemain* which was Mackintosh's manner, laying his open hand flat and coldly against yours. The *high official*, the Archbishop of York's, who carries your hand aloft on a level with his forehead. The *rural* or *vigorous* shake, &c., &c.

DESCRIBING the *dining* process by which people in London extract all they can from new literary lions, Smith was irresistibly comic : Here's a new man of genius arrived ; put on the stew-pan, fry away ; we'll soon get it all out of him.

THE liberality of churchmen generally, is like the quantity of matter in a cone—both get less and less as they move higher and higher.

SOMEONE at a dinner party sitting next to Sydney Smith was talking of the value of some landed property, and saying it was worth five pounds a foot per annum. "Ah !" said Smith, "the price of a London footman six foot high—thirty guineas a year."

DISCUSSING a recent geological work, Sydney Smith asked his listeners to imagine an excavation at some distant date on the site of St Paul's, a lecture by the Owen of a future age on the thigh-bone of a minor Canon, or the tooth of a Dean,—the form, qualities, the knowledge, tastes, propensities, he would discover from them.

WE naturally lose illusions as we get older, like teeth, but there is no one to fit a new set into our understandings. I have, alas! only one illusion left, and that is the Archbishop of Canterbury.

—◇◇◇—

LADY HOLLAND was of a somewhat imperious nature, even with the great men who foregathered at Holland House, and her manner justified Smith's retort, when she said to him, "Sydney, ring the bell."

"Oh yes!" he answered, "and shall I sweep the room?"

—◇◇◇—

SOMEONE speaking of the utility of a certain measure, and quoting a friend's opinion in support of it, Sydney Smith broke in saying—

"Yes, he is of the utilitarian school. That man is so hard you might drive a broad-wheeled wagon over him, and it would produce no impression; if you were to bore holes in him with a gimlet, I am convinced sawdust would come out of him. That school treat mankind as if they were mere machines; the feelings or affections never enter into their calculations. If everything is to be sacrificed to utility, why do you bury your grandmother at all? Why don't you cut her into small pieces at once, and make portable soup of her?"

THE Hon. Mrs Norton was fanning Sydney Smith when he suddenly asked, "Is Eastlake here? What a picture he would make! Beauty fanning Piety—happy Piety!"

SMITH once laughingly described his friends in the next world. Of Cornewall Lewis he said, "If he ever does go to Hades, his punishment will be to sit book-less for ever,

treaty-less, pamphlet-less, grammar-less; in vain will he implore the Bishop of London, sitting aloft, to send him one little treatise on the Greek article, or one smallest dissertation on the verbs in $\mu\iota$."

GOUT is the only enemy which I don't wish to have at my feet.

SYDNEY SMITH spoke of a certain kind of charity as "the integumental charity that covers so many sins."

AT a large dinner at Holland House, Sydney Smith met a French *savant*, who took it upon himself to annoy the best disposed of the company by a variety of freethinking speculations.

"Very good soup this!" slyly struck in Smith.

"*Oui, monsieur, c'est excellente!*"

"Pray, sir," was the retort, which for that time and place was worth a library of argument, "do you believe in a cook?"

COMING suddenly upon the great Jeffrey of *Edinburgh* fame riding upon the children's donkey, Smith hailed him thus—

> Witty as Horatius Flaccus,
> As great a Jacobin as Gracchus,
> Short, though not as fat as Bacchus,
> Riding on a little Jackass.

THERE is a New Zealand attorney just arrived in London, with 6s. 8d. tattooed all over his face.

SYDNEY SMITH, sitting by a brother clergy-man at dinner, observed afterwards that his dull neighbour had a *twelve-parson power* of conversation.

—⌇∿∿⌇—

THE Archbishop of York, an accomplished rider, said to Sydney, who could not ride at all, " I hear, Mr Smith, you do not approve of much riding for the clergy."

" Why, my lord," replied he, " perhaps there is not *much* objection, provided they do not ride too well, and stick out their toes pro-fessionally."

—⌇∿∿⌇—

ONE day the conversation turned upon an obstinate man who was full of prejudices. Sydney Smith, who knew his character and opinions, expressed despair, saying, "You might as well attempt to poultice the humps off a camel's back."

—⌇∿∿⌇—

JEFFREY, Sydney Smith, and other friends paid a visit to Deville, the phrenologist, *incog.*

" This gentleman's case," said Deville, feeling Smith's bumps, "is clear enough. His faculties are those of a naturalist, and I see that he gratifies them. This gentleman is always happy among his collection of birds and fishes."

"Sir," said Sydney Smith, turning round upon him solemnly with open eyes, "I don't know a fish from a bird."

※

MRS MARCET was on a visit at Foston, and on showing her round, Smith said, "I am a great doctor; would you like to hear some of my medicines?"

"Oh yes, Mr Sydney."

"Well, then there is the Gentle-jog, a pleasure to take it; the Bulldog, for more serious cases; Peter's Puke; Heart's Delight, the comfort of all the old women in the village; Rub-a-dub, a capital embrocation; Dead-stop, settles the matter at once; Up-with-it-then, needs no explanation."

The visitor was then taken downstairs, and entered a room filled entirely on one side with medicines, and on the other with every description of groceries, and household or agricultural necessaries; in the centre, a large chest forming

a table, and divided into compartments for
soap, candles, salt, and sugar.

"Here you see," said Smith, spreading out
his hands and laughing, "every human want
before you,—

"Man wants but little here below,
As beef, veal, mutton, pork, lamb, venison show!"

SYDNEY SMITH described his arriving late
at a dinner, and how everyone was engaged, "and there was Hallam with his mouth
full of cabbage and contradiction."

WHEN informed that his daughter's
marriage had been announced in the
London papers, under *Fashionable Intelligence*,
Sydney Smith exclaimed with a merry twinkle
in his eye, "How absurd!—Why, we pay our
bills!"

TWO young ladies entering a drawing-room,
someone remarked to Sydney Smith what
a pretty contrast their different styles of beauty

made. " Yes," responded he, " Miss L. reminds me of a youthful Minerva; and her friend, as a doctor's daughter must, you know, be the Venus de Medicis."

A T a large dinner party, the death of Dugald Stewart was announced. The news was received with so much levity by a lady of rank, who sat by Sydney Smith, that he turned round to her saying, "Madam, when we are told of the death of so great a man as Mr Dugald Stewart, it is usual in civilised society, to look grave for at least the space of five seconds."

S YDNEY SMITH said in one of his writings that a false quantity at the commencement of the career of a young man intended for public life, was rarely got over; when a lady asked him what a false quantity was, he explained it to be in a man the same as a *faux pas* in a woman.

SYDNEY SMITH—

" CORRESPONDENCES," said Smith to a friend who complained about having had no letters during a temporary absence, "are like small clothes before the invention of suspenders—it is impossible to keep them up."

A N argument arose in which Sydney Smith observed how many of the most eminent men of the world had been diminutive in person, and after naming several among the ancients, he added, "Why, look there, at Jeffrey; and there is my little friend D—, who has not body enough to cover his mind decently with; his intellect is improperly exposed."

—◦◦◦◦◦◦—

S YDNEY SMITH drolly described his friends during an influenza epidemic, "and poor Hallam was tossing and tumbling in his bed when the watchman came by and called 'twelve o'clock and a starlight night.'

"Here was an opportunity for controversy when it seemed most out of the question! Up Hallam jumped with, 'I question that, — I question that! Starlight! I see a star, I admit; but I doubt whether that constitutes starlight.'

"Hours more of tossing and tumbling; and then comes the watchman again: 'Past two o'clock, and a cloudy morning.'

"'I question that,—I question that,' says Hallam, and he rushes to the window and throws up the sash—influenza notwithstanding. 'Watchman! do you mean to call this a cloudy morning? I see a star. And I question its being past two o'clock—I question it, I question it.'"

LESLIE, the Scotch philosopher, had called upon Jeffrey, just as the latter was going out riding, to ask him to explain some point concerning the North Pole. Jeffrey, who was in a hurry, exclaimed as he rode off, "Oh! damn the North Pole!"

This Leslie complained of to Sydney Smith, who entered gravely into his feelings, and told

him in confidence, that he himself had once heard Jeffrey *speak disrespectfully of the Equator*.

—◦◦◦—

OH, dear me, yes, you find people ready enough to do the Samaritan—without the oil and twopence.

THERE being a rumour that in the event of certain " Church Reforms," all the church dignitaries would resign, Smith drew a picture of the sad state the country would be in ; having to send to America to borrow a bishop : " Have you such a thing as a bishop you could lend us? Shall keep him only a fortnight, and return him with a new cassock," &c.

WHEN Lord John Russell went to Exeter after the defeat of the Reform Bill, the people along the road were much disappointed at his smallness. Sydney Smith told them that he was much bigger before the Bill was thrown out, but he was reduced by excessive anxiety about the people. This we are told brought tears to their eyes.

SMITH, when he became Canon of St Paul's, retained his Bristol appointment, and described his alternation from town to country as —dining with the rich in London, and physicking the poor in the country ; passing from the sauce of Dives to the sores of Lazarus.

MY idea of heaven is, eating *foie gras* to the sound of trumpets.

DESCRIBING his home-life at Foston-le-Clay, Sydney Smith told how, on *state* occasions his carpenter, Jack Robinson, took off his apron and waited at table, and did pretty well too, though he sometimes naturally made a mistake, and stuck a gimlet into the bread instead of a fork.

WHILE suffering from illness, during which, however, his playfulness never left him, Sydney Smith said that he felt so weak that he verily believed, if the knife were put into his hand he should not have strength or energy enough to stick it in a Dissenter.

—ᴧᴧᴧᴧᴧ—

WHEN there was a rumour that Rogers was to be married, Sydney Smith, who never tired of making fun out of the cadaverous poet, suggested the two Miss Berrys as bridesmaids, the sexton as best-man, and the Rev. Mr Coffin (a clergyman known at that time in London) as the proper person to officiate at the wedding, which would of course take place in the Church of St Sepulchre.

DESCRIBING the starting of the *Edinburgh Review*, Sydney Smith said, " I proposed that we should set up a Review. This was acceded to with acclamation. I was appointed editor, and remained long enough in Edinburgh to edit the first number of the Review. The motto I proposed for the Review was—

' *Tenui Musam meditamur avenâ.*'

' We cultivate literature on a little oatmeal.'

But this was too near the truth to be admitted ; so we took our present grave motto from Publius Syrus, of whom none of us had, I am sure, read a single line."

—*∿∿*—

NOW I mean not to drink one drop of wine to-day, and I shall be mad with spirits. I always am when I drink no wine. It is curious the effect a thimbleful of wine has upon me ; I feel as flat as A.'s jokes ; it destroys my understanding. I forget the numbers of the Muses,--and think them thirty-nine, of course ; and only get myself right again by repeating the lines "Descend ye thirty-nine," and finding it two feet too long.

—*∿∿*—

DESCRIBING Nether Avon (near Salisbury), the scene of his first curacy, Smith spoke of it as a pretty feature in a *plain* face.

SMITH spoke of the Archdeacon of Newfoundland as a man who sits bobbing for
cod, and pocketing every tenth fish.

DANIEL O'CONNELL presented Sydney
Smith to his friends, saying, "Allow me

to introduce to you the ancient defender of our
faith."

Sydney laughingly interrupted him, saying,
"Of your *cause*, if you please ; *not* of your
faith."

SCOTLAND is only the *knuckle* end of England.

—◦◦◦—

TALLEYRAND was to be found so constantly at Holland House that Sydney Smith said anyone was sure of being Talleyranded there.

—◦◦◦—

SMITH described a dinner at his publishers' (Longmans'): Rees carving *plerumque secat res.*

—◦◦◦—

TALKING of the bad effects of late hours, Sydney Smith remarked of some distinguished diner out that there would be on his tomb, "He dined late—" "and died early," added Luttrell.

—◦◦◦—

LORD LANSDOWNE having promised to accompany Tom Moore to some Roman Catholic religious establishment, Smith charged Moore with a design upon Lansdowne's orthodoxy, and recommended that there should be some sound Protestant tracts put up with the sandwiches in the carriage.

THERE arose a discussion on the *Inferno* of
Dante, and the tortures he had invented.

"He may be a great poet," said Sydney
Smith, "but as to inventing tortures, I consider
him a mere bungler, — no imagination — no
knowledge of the human heart. If I had taken
it in hand, I would show you what torture
really was. For instance (turning to his friend,
Mrs Marcet), you should be doomed to listen
for a thousand years to conversations between
Caroline and Emily, where Caroline should

always give wrong explanations in chemistry,
and Emily in the end be unable to distinguish
an acid from an alkali.

"You, Macaulay, let me consider—oh, you
should be dumb. False dates and facts of the
reign of Queen Anne should for ever be shouted
in your ears, all liberal and honest opinions
should be ridiculed in your presence; and you

should not be able to say a single word during that period in their defence."

· "And what would you condemn me to, Mr Smith?" said a young mother.

"Why you should for ever see those three sweet little girls of yours on the point of falling downstairs, and never be able to save them. There—what tortures are there in Dante equal to these?"

DON'T you know, as the French say, there are three sexes—men, women, and clergymen.

LADY CORK was once so moved by a charity sermon, that she begged me to lend her a guinea for her contribution. I did so. She never repaid me, and spent it on herself.

UNDER the last regimen of his physician, Sydney Smith exclaimed to a friend, "Ah! Charles, I wish I were allowed to eat even the wing of a roasted butterfly."

WHAT a pity it is that in England we have no amusements but vice and religion.

WHEN I began to thump the cushion of my pulpit on first coming to Foston, as is my wont when I preach, the accumulated dust of a hundred and fifty years made such a cloud, that for some minutes I lost sight of my congregation.

" WE *were* savage," said Smith, recalling the early days of the *Edinburgh Review.* " I remember how Brougham and I sat trying one night how we could exasperate our cruelty to the utmost. We had got hold of a poor nervous little vegetarian, who had put out a poor silly little book, and when we had done our review of it, we sat trying to find one more chink, one more crevice, through which we might drop in one more drop of verjuice to eat into his bones."

HOLDING forth to a laughing circle on the subject of tithes and the *Tripartite* division, Sydney Smith said, " I am sorry to tell you that the great historian, Hallam, has declared himself in favour of the Tripartite, and contends that it was so, in the age of King Fiddlefred ; but we of the Church," he continued, slapping his breast mock-heroically, " say, 'a fig for King Fiddlefred ; we will keep our tithes to ourselves.' "

DANTE in his Purgatorio would have assigned five hundred years of *assenting* to Hallam, and as many to Rogers of *praising* his fellow-creatures.

—∿∿∿—

TALKING of absence of mind—the oddest instance of absence of mind happened to me once in forgetting my own name. I knocked at a door in London ; asked, Is Mr B. at home? "Yes, sir, pray what name shall I say?"

I looked into the man's face astonished : "What name? what name? Ay, that is the question. What is my name?"

I believe the man thought me mad, but it is literally true, that during the space of two or three minutes, I had no more idea of who I was than if I had never existed. I did not know whether I was a Dissenter or a layman. I felt as dull as Sternhold and Hopkins. At last,  to my great relief, it flashed across me that I was Sydney Smith.

—∿∿∿—

I HEARD of a clergyman who went jogging along the road till he came to a turnpike— "What is to pay?"

"Pay, sir, for what?" asked the turnpike man.

"Why, for my horse to be sure."

"Your horse, sir? What horse? There is no horse, sir."

"No horse? God bless me!" said he, suddenly looking down between his legs, "I thought I was on horseback."

—∿∿∿—

SYDNEY SMITH said he was magnanimous, when talking to Tom Moore and Miss Berry, in avowing that he had never before heard of Lamartine. Was it another name for the blacking man! Because, if so, he's Martin here, La-Martine in France, and Martin Luther in Germany.

—∿∿∿—

A FRIEND having said that bread was about to be made from sawdust, Sydney Smith imagined that people would soon have *sprigs* coming out of them. Young ladies dressing for a ball, would say, "Mamma, I'm beginning to sprout."

—∿∿∿—

SUGGESTED derivations of words being offered at a party, Smith gave nincompoop, from *non compos;* cock-a-whoop, from the taking the cock out of a barrel of ale, and setting it on the hoop to let the ale flow merrily.

TALKING of the mixture of character in O'Connell, Sydney Smith summed up all by saying, "The only way to deal with such a man is to hang him up, and erect a statue to him under his gallows."

—◦◇◇◦—

SYDNEY SMITH'S advice to a writer in composing was :—"As a general rule, run your pen through every other word you have written ; you have no idea what vigour it will give your style."

—◦◇◇◦—

PREACHING a charity sermon, Sydney Smith frequently repeated the assertion that, of all nations, the English were most distinguished for generosity and the love of their species. The collection was less than he expected, and he said that he had evidently made a great mistake, and that his expression should have been that they were distinguished for the love of their *specie*.

—◦◇◇◦—

SOME young person answering on a subject in discussion, "I don't know that, Mr Smith."

"Ah, what you don't know would make a great book," he said, smiling.

A DISCUSSION took place as to whether it was better to hear or read Macaulay. Rogers said, "the former, because you need not listen."

"Oh, I'm for the latter," said Sydney Smith, "because you can't dog's-ear and interline him and put him on the shelf when he is talking."

—⁓⋀⋁⋀⋁⁓—

I DELIGHT in a stage coach and four, and how could I have gone by one as Bishop? I might have found myself with a young lady  of strong Dissenting principles, who would have called for help to disgrace the Church ; or with an Atheist, who told me what he had in his heart ; and when I had taken refuge on the out- side, I might have found an Unitarian in the basket ; or if I got on the box, the coachman might have told me that "he was once one of those rascally parsons, but had now taken to a better and an honester trade."

—⁓⋀⋁⋀⋁⁓—

" IF you Whigs send Campbell, Lord Chan- cellor to Ireland, you will drive them mad," said a friend.

"And a very short stage to go, my lord," replied Smith, "and no postilions to pay."

THEY now speak of the peculiar difficulties
and restrictions of the episcopal office.
I only read in Scripture of two inhibitions—
boxing and polygamy.

—◡◡◡◡—

SOON after Lord Lyndhurst became Lord
Chancellor, Sydney Smith, who was on
intimate terms with him, was present at a
dinner party at his house. The conversation
turned to the custom in India of widows burning themselves in their husbands' funeral pyre.
For the sake of the argument, Smith began to
defend the practice, and asserted that no wife
who truly loved her husband could wish to
survive him.

"But if Lord Lyndhurst were to die, you
would be sorry that Lady Lyndhurst should
burn herself?" was the sudden and embarrass-
ing question of one of the guests.

"Lady Lyndhurst," came the deliberate
reply "would, no doubt, as an affectionate
wife, consider it her duty to burn herself, but
it would be our duty to put her out ; and, as
the wife of the Lord Chancellor, Lady Lyndhurst should not be put out like an ordinary
widow. It should be a State affair. First, a
procession of the judges, then of the lawyers—"

"But pray, Mr Smith, where are the clergy?"

"All gone to congratulate the new Lord
Chancellor," came the sly response.

BABBAGE always seems at white heat, ready to scorch up some rival man of science.

ON having some things charged at the Customs House, Smith enquired, " Under what head?"

" Unmentioned articles," was the reply.

" I suppose, then, you would tax the Thirty-nine?"

" IN the country!" exclaimed Sydney Smith. "Oh, in the country I always fear that creation will expire before tea-time."

THE Archbishop of York having met with an accident, " Yes," said Smith, " he has sprained the *tendo Athanasii*, which in laymen is the *tendo Achillis*."

SMITH once gave a neat definition of a " card-sharper,"—" One who sells ' correct cards,' and gets sent to jail because they rove incorrect."

AFTER attending Lady Essex's private theatricals, Sydney Smith said that he watched with intense anxiety for the slightest approach of impropriety, that he might carry off the Archbishop of York as the pious Æneas did his sire.

—√√√√—

AN officer having been publicly reproved by the Duke of Wellington, Sydney Smith said, " He can't live, you know ; his wife and

children will be always in tears, his pointers will bite him, the pew opener won't give him a seat, the butcher won't trust him, his horse will always kick him off—prussic acid will be too good for him."

N O railroad will be safe until they have made a Bishop *in partibus.*

—∿∧∨∧∿—

A MEMBER of Parliament having said that if the Corn Laws were repealed, " we should return to the food of our ancestors," some friend asked Smith, " What did he mean ? "

" Thistles, to be sure," was the reply.

—∿∧∨∧∿—

S YDNEY SMITH having offered to call somewhere, was told, " Do, we shall be on our knees to you, if you come."

" I'm glad to hear it," he replied, " I like to see you in that attitude, as it brings me in several hundreds a year."

—∿∧∨∧∿—

N EVER gamble at the game of life ; be content to play for sixpences ; marriage is too high a stake for a wise man to risk.

—∿∧∨∧∿—

S AID Smith to Mrs Grote, " Go where you will, do what you please, I have the most perfect confidence in your *indiscretion.*"

SYDNEY SMITH once called the railway whistle, "the attorney," because it is suggestive of the shriek of a spirit in torment, "and we have no right to assume that any other class of men is damned."

—⁄∿∿⁄—

A LADY told Smith that Macaulay had not talked quite so much as usual.

"Why, my dear, how could he? Whenever I gave him a chance, you cut in."

—⁄∿∿⁄—

AN acquaintance of Sydney Smith's had been platitudinising about the value of travel —he of course having travelled—and at length said, "Do you see this stick, sir? This stick has been all round the world."

"Indeed," said Smith, "and yet it *is only a stick.*"

—⁄∿∿⁄—

SMITH spoke of the knowledge sailors have of ships at a great distance; took them off, saying, with a telescope to the eye, "Damn her, she's the 'Delight,' laden with tallow!"

"THE entertainment of the clergy," Sydney Smith described as, "that most solemn and terrible duty of a Bishop."

—⁓⋀⋁⋀⋎—

SOMEONE having remarked upon the wonderful improvement in a friend since his success. "Ah!" exclaimed Sydney Smith, " Praise is the best diet for us after all."

—⁓⋀⋁⋀⋎—

OF the court of Chancery, Sydney Smith said that it was like a boa constrictor ; it swallowed up the estates of English gentlemen in haste, and digested them at leisure.

—⁓⋀⋁⋀⋎—

A FRIEND asked Sydney Smith what was Puseyism.

" Puseyism, sir," replied the witty Canon, " is inflexion and genuflexion ; posture and imposture ; bowing to the east, and curtseying to the west."

—⁓⋀⋁⋀⋎—

WHY are old Tories like last year's walnuts? Because they are troublesome to *Peel*.

WHEN Sydney Smith got the prebendal stall in our cathedral (a Bristolian recounts the story), he was lodging in College Green ; and as his fame as a convivialist was not then so noised and known as subsequently, he was allowed to dine at home more frequently than one would suppose ; and his dinner was always a beefsteak, and that beefsteak he always bought himself. I was then my own purveyor, and there were few days when he was in residence that I did not meet him at Burge's in Denmark Street (his favourite butcher, and mine), overseeing and selecting his own cut. After Sydney had described a

 circle with his finger round a certain pin-bone, and emphatically told the man of fat to "cut there, and cut boldly," as the Roman augur said, Burge turned to me and asked, "And where will you be helped, sir ? "

"I'll follow suit," said I, "the cut next to Mr Smith's. I can't go wrong with such a precedent."

The Canon's droll eye twinkled ; his large, pouting, and somewhat luxurious lip moved with that comic twitch that spoke the man, as he said, "You're a wise man, sir ; this is one of the cases where you can't err if you follow the Church, and you'll find your obedience rewarded with a good beefsteak."

SPEAKING of a noble lord, someone said that he must have felt himself astonished at becoming the father of a clever son.

"Yes," said Sydney Smith, "he must have felt like a hen who has hatched a duck, and sees it suddenly take to the water."

—◦◦◦—

PASSING through a bye-street behind St Paul's, Sydney Smith heard two women abusing each other from opposite houses. "They will never agree," said he, "for they argue from different premises."

—◦◦◦—

SYDNEY SMITH said of a hospitable friend of his in the Highlands, that he could always tell the state of the weather by the quantity of whiskey drunk in his house during the day; averring that the glass went up in the hand as the mercury went down in the hall.

—◦◦◦—

A COUNTRY squire having been worsted in an argument with Sydney Smith, took his revenge by remarking, "If I had a son who was an idiot, by Jove, I'd make him a parson."

"Very probably," said Sydney Smith, "but I see that your father was of a different mind."

AT a public dinner, three gentlemen having at the same moment stood up for the purpose of saying grace, Sydney Smith, who was present, called them " the three Graces."

LORD JOHN RUSSELL, remarkable for the smallness of his person, as Lord Nugent was for the reverse, was expected at a house where Sydney Smith was a guest.

"Lord John comes here to-day," said Sydney Smith ; " his corporeal anti-part, Lord Nugent,

is already here. Heaven send he may not *swallow John !* There are, however, stomach pumps in case of accident."

COUNTRY life is very good ; in fact, the best—for cattle.

SPEAKING of a lady's smile, Sydney Smith said it was so radiant that it would force a gooseberry bush into flower.

—◇◇◇◇—

OF three sisters, Sydney Smith said that they were all so beautiful that Paris could not have decided between them.

—◇◇◇◇—

AT one of the Holland House dinner parties, Crockford's Club, then forming, was talked of, and the noble hostess observed that the female passion for diamonds was surely less ruinous than the rage for play among men.

"In short, you think," said Rogers, "that clubs are worse than diamonds."

This excited a laugh, and when it had subsided, Sydney Smith wrote the following impromptu most appropriately on *a card*—

"Thoughtless that 'all that's brightest fades,'
Unmindful of the *Knave of Spades*,
    The Sexton and his Subs :
How foolishly we play our parts !
Our wives on *diamonds* set their *hearts*,
    And we our *hearts* on *clubs !*"

WHEN a body of horse guards were passing, Sydney Smith turned to an officer who was standing by him (Lord William Russell), saying, "I suppose you must now feel the same in looking at those that I do in looking at a congregation."

—◊◊◊—

BOBUS SMITH and Sir Henry Holland were talking of the comparative merits of the learned professions in affording agreeable members of society.

"Your profession (the law), for instance, certainly does not make angels of men," said Sir Henry.

"No," quietly answered Bobus, as he glanced with an innocent air at the physician, "no—but yours does!"

—◊◊◊—

TOM MOORE mentioned Kean's having eked out his means of living before he emerged into celebrity by teaching dancing, fencing, elocution, and box-ing.

"*Elocution and boxing*," echoed Bobus Smith, "a word and a blow."

WILKIE was looking over "H.B.'s" early
sketches, and admiring some of them
as works of art, when, pointing to a bit in one
of them, he said, "That really reminds me of
Titian."

"*Poli*tician!" exclaimed Bobus.

R. Brinsley Sheridan.

SHERIDAN.

BON-MOTS

OF

SHERIDAN.

WHILE at Harrow, we are told, Sheridan was made a frequent butt for the ridicule of the other boys, particularly those who were born of great families, or to brighter prospects. One of the most troublesome and impertinent of these youths, the son of an eminent physician in London, took occasion in the playground to exercise his wit at the expense of Sheridan, as being the son of a player. Sheridan, however, quickly retorted, " ' Tis true, my father lives by pleasing people, but yours lives by killing them."

ONE day, meeting two royal dukes walking up St James's Street, Sheridan was thus addressed by the younger, "I say, Sherry, we have just been discussing whether you are a greater fool or rogue. What is your own opinion, my boy?"

Sheridan, having bowed and smiled at the compliment, took each of them by an arm, and instantly replied, "Why, i' faith, I believe I am between *both*."

—ᴧᴧᴧᴧ—

LOOKING over a number of the *Quarterly Review* one day at Brookes's, Sheridan said, in reply to a gentleman who observed that the editor, Gifford, had boasted of his power of conferring and distributing literary reputation, "Very likely, and in the present instance I think he has done it so profusely as to have left none for himself."

—ᴧᴧᴧᴧ—

A DRURY LANE after-piece was chiefly remarkable for the introduction of a wonderful performing dog, and Sheridan and a friend went to see the performance. As they entered the green-room, Dignum (who played in the piece) said to Sheridan with a woful countenance—

"Sir, there is no guarding against illness : it is truly lamentable to stop the run of a successful piece like this ; but really—"

"Really what?" cried Sheridan, interrupting him.

"I am so unwell that I cannot go on longer than to-night."

"You!" exclaimed Sheridan, "my good fellow, you terrified me; I thought you were going to say that the dog was taken ill."

B URKE in early life had attended a debating society, which used to meet at a certain baker's. On a memorable occasion in the House

of Commons, he said, "I quit the camp," and crossing over from the Opposition took his seat on the Ministerial benches, whence he rose and made a brillant speech against his ci-devant friends.

Sheridan, annoyed at the defection, said, "The

honourable gentleman, to quote his own expression, has quitted the camp; he will recollect that he quitted it as a deserter, and I sincerely hope he will never attempt to return as a spy; but I, for one, cannot sympathise in the astonishment with which an act of apostacy so flagrant has electrified the House; for neither I, nor the honourable gentleman, have forgotten whence he obtained the weapons which he now uses against us: so far from being at all astonished at the honourable gentleman's tergiversation, I consider it not only characteristic, but consistent, that he who in the outset of life made so extraordinary a blunder as to go to a baker's for eloquence, should finish such a career by coming to the House of Commons to get bread."

—◦◦◦◦◦◦—

AT the close of Sheridan's unsuccessful Westminster contest, it was hoped that his noble Caledonian opponent (Lord Cochrane) would drown the memory of differences in a friendly bottle.

"With all my heart," said Sheridan, "and will thank his lordship to make it a Scotch pint."

—◦◦◦◦◦◦—

WHEN Sheridan was asked what wine he liked best, he said—other people's.

I N describing the cavern scene of Coleridge's *Remorse*, as produced at Drury Lane, Sheridan said it was "drip, drip, drip—nothing but dripping."

—⁓⋀⋁⁓—

TOWARDS the close of the Westminster election, when all the exertions of Sheridan's friends had failed to secure his return, he bore his defeat with good humour. A sailor, anxious to view the proceedings, had climbed one of the supports in front of the hustings. As Sheridan commenced his speech, his eye fell upon the tar aloft, and he turned the incident to ludicrous account by saying that had he but other five hundred voters as upright as the perpendicular gentleman before him, they would yet place him where *he* was— *at the head of the pole!*

—⁓⋀⋁⁓—

CUMBERLAND, the irritable opponent of all merit but his own, was with his young family at an early performance of the *School for Scandal;* they were seated in the stage-box.

the little children screamed with delight, but the less easily pleased fretful author pinched them, exclaiming, " What are you laughing at, my dear little folks? you should not laugh, my angels, there is nothing to laugh at!" and then, in an undertone, " Keep still, you little dunces." When Sheridan was told of this, he said, "it was ungrateful of Cumberland to have been displeased with his children for laughing at my comedy, for when I went to see his tragedy I laughed from beginning to end."

—∿∿∿—

TO Lord Holland Sheridan said one day: " They talk of avarice, lust, ambition, as great passions. Vanity is the great commanding passion of all. It is this that produces the most grand and heroic deeds, or impels to the most dreadful crimes. Save me from this passion, and I can defy the others. They are mere urchins, but this is a giant."

—∿∿∿—

SHERIDAN was once talking to a friend about the Prince Regent, who took great credit to himself for various public occurrences, as if they had been directed by his political skill, or foreseen by his political sagacity; "but," said Sheridan, after expatiating on this, " what his Royal Highness more particularly prides himself upon, is the late excellent harvest."

AN unfortunate dramatist whose comedies, when returned upon his hands, were generally reduced by the managers from five acts to two, or even one, complained in wrath and bitterness to Sheridan, who attempted to console him by saying, " Why, my good fellow, what I would advise you is, to present a comedy of a *score* of acts, and the devil will be in it if *five* be not saved."

—◦◦◦◦—

WHEN seated at his window not long before his death, seeing a hearse go by, Sheridan exclaimed, " Ah, that is the carriage *after all!*"

—◦◦◦◦—

SHAW, having lent Sheridan five hundred pounds, dunned him for it. One day, after rating Sheridan, he said he must have the money. Sheridan, having played off some of his plausible wheedling upon him, ended by saying that he was very much in want of twenty-five pounds to pay the expenses of a journey he was about to take, and he knew Shaw would be good-natured enough to lend it to him.

" 'Pon my word," said Shaw, " this is too bad ; after keeping me out of my money in so shameful a manner you now have the face to ask me for more ; but it won't do—it is most disgraceful, and I must have my money."

" My dear fellow," replied Sheridan, " do

hear reason ; the sum you ask *me* for is a very considerable one ; whereas I only ask *you* for five and twenty pounds ! "

—◡◠◡—

A FRIENDLY wine merchant, Challie, was dining with Sheridan when a noble visitor invited the wit down to his country place for the shooting season. Sheridan said that he was sorry not to be able to accept the invitation, assuming, as one of his reasons, that his friend Challie had determined on *keeping him in port* for the rest of the season. " By-the-bye, Challie," said Sheridan playfully, " you would make a capital banker ! "

" A banker ! " echoed Challie, laughing heartily at the idea ; " a banker, Mr Sheridan ! why so ? a banker and a wine merchant ? "

" The exact thing, my dear friend ; for uniting the business of the wine merchant and banker, you could manage a capital business : since for those who took your *draughts* overnight you could reciprocate by honouring their *drafts* in the morning."

ONE day a creditor came into Sheridan's room for a bill, and found him seated before a table on which two or three hundred pounds in gold and notes were strewed.

"It's no use looking at that, my good fellow," said Sheridan, "that is all bespoken for debts of honour."

"Very well," replied the tradesman, tearing up his security and throwing it on the fire, "now mine is a debt of honour."

"So it is, and must be paid at once," said Sheridan, handing him over the money.

CANNING had nicknamed Lord Sidmouth *the Doctor*, he being the son of a physician, an intimate friend of the great Lord Chatham. When the Scotch members deserted the Addington Ministry upon a trying vote, Sheridan said to the Premier, across the table of the House, "Doctor! the Thanes fly from thee!"

WHEN Garrick retired from Drury Lane, and sold his half interest in the theatre, Sheridan purchased two-fifths of that half for ten thousand pounds. All his friends and acquaintances were curious to know how he got the money ; all kinds of rumours were rife, and one friend went so far as to ask the dramatist point blank where the money came from.

"Your importunities have prevailed," at length replied Sheridan, with a convulsive effort, assuming an extraordinary gravity of manner, and with a tremulous, subdued, half-suppressed voice, expressive of greatest agitation, "and your curiosity must be gratified, but I had hoped to have kept the secret confined within my own breast, and to have borne with its consuming fires even to the grave."

"Mr Sheridan, I—I really do not wish," exclaimed the other, but he was interrupted ere the sentence could be concluded by the stern theatrical air and gesture of Sheridan, as he advanced towards him.

"Ay, sir, to the grave, where we might both have mouldered and been forgotten."

"Really, and seriously, Mr Sheridan, I have no desire to inquire into your secrets."

"But you have forced it from me, and involved yourself in inextricable danger. Be the peril, therefore, on your own head, since you have obtained from me a confession which no tongue should utter or ear should hear, and which must necessarily involve yourself, by the keeping of my secret, in my guilt."

"Mr Sheridan, this is really too serious a matter—I beg your pardon—I really must beg your pardon, and—good morning."

"Stay, stay ; yet hold—let us see that we are not observed, that no eavesdropper catch the sound of our voices, or carry away the startling evidence of our daring."

" What in the name of heaven, Mr Sheridan, do you allude to ? "

" Heaven has nothing to do with the damning deed ! "

The friend, paralysed, sunk almost fainting in his chair, with the smell of brimstone in his nostrils, and the configuration of Friar Bacon floating before his eyes. Sheridan approached the door of the apartment with slow and measured step, and holding the handle, turned suddenly round upon his bewildered friend— " Swear ! swear ! " he cried, " never to reveal my secret ! "

" Oh, I never will, positively— upon my honour, never."

" I am satisfied. Well then,"—pausing for a moment, and assuming great anguish with remorse depicted on his countenance, he con- tinued, "since it must be so, I have discovered," —and elevating his voice to the highest pitch, he roared out,—"the philosopher's stone ! " saying which, he darted out of the room, banging the door after him, and leaving his

I

bewildered auditor to revolve the matter in his own mind, and digest it as he could. Sheridan was a capital actor in his own jokes, and it was a capital joke.

—◌◌◌—

SHERIDAN, with his son Tom, was dining one day at Peter Moore's, Tom being then in a nervous debilitated state. The servant, in passing quickly between the guests and the fire-place struck down the plate warmer. This made a strange rattle, and caused Tom Sheridan to start and tremble. Peter Moore, provoked at this, rebuked the servant and said, '' I suppose you have broken all the plates ? ''

'' No, sir,'' said the servant, '' not one.''

'' No ? '' exclaimed Sheridan, '' then, damn it, you have made all that noise for nothing.''

—◌◌◌—

AT one of Sheridan's Parliamentary election contests, a person on horseback had penetrated the crowd near the hustings, when the horse became restive, and there was a loud outcry against the intrusion. While some strove to appease the clamour, others urged Sheridan to proceed.

'' Gentlemen,'' replied he, '' when the chorus of *The Horse and his Rider* is finished, I shall continue.''

ON the subject of the liberty of the press (in 1810) Sheridan was very eloquent when he exclaimed of his opponents in Parliament :— " Give them a corrupt House of Lords ; give them a venal House of Commons ; give them a tyrannical Prince ; give them a truckling court,—and let me have an unfettered press ; I will defy them to encroach a hair's-breadth upon the liberties of England."

—–√∿∿—

IT is said that Sheridan never gave Monk Lewis any of the profits of *The Castle Spectre*. One day Monk Lewis being in company with him, said, " Sheridan, I will make you a large bet."

Sheridan, who was always ready to make a wager, asked eagerly, " What bet ? "

" All the profits of *Castle Spectre*," said Lewis.

" I will tell you what," retorted Sheridan, " I will make you a very small one —what it is worth."

—√∿∿—

THE HON. Mr S. having finished a tragedy, sent it to Sheridan for performance at Drur Lane. The proprietor looked at it, and

laid it on the table.   In a few days the author
called.

"Well now, my dear Sheridan, pray what
do you think of it?   My friend Cumberland
has promised me a prologue ; and I dare say,
for the interest of the theatre, you will have no
objection to supply me with an epilogue?"

"Trust me, my dear sir," replied Sheridan
drily, "it will never come to that, depend on 't."

THE chronic state of money difficulties in
which Sheridan was situated is notorious.
At one time, Hanson, a furnishing ironmonger,
was rather a heavy creditor, so was Gunter, the
confectioner, but for a much smaller amount.
Gunter had sent in his bill, demanding immediate payment, on the morning when Hanson
called for settlement of his own.   Gunter's bill
lay upon the table.   Hanson was pressing,
Sheridan equally apologetic.

"But I must have my account settled, Mr
Sheridan ; promises are not payment, and I
cannot wait any longer."

"Well, my dear sir, if you can show me the
way how to settle it, I shall most cheerfully
comply with your wishes," was the calm reply.

"Me show you," retorted Hanson, "how am
I to know your resources?"

"You know Gunter? perhaps you will have

no objection to take his bill," said Sheridan, with a merriment in his eye, as the comical thought struck him, while glancing at the paper on the table.

"Not at all; I know Gunter to be a safe, good man."

"Well then," handing the folded paper over to the expectant tradesman, "there's his bill—take it, make what use of it you can, and when you have done with it, I must beg of you to

return it receipted," and, bowing politely, he left the bewildered Hanson to the acceptance or rejection of the joke, as might best suit his fancy.

—⌇⋏⋏⋏⋏—

IN the House of Commons Pitt rallied Sheridan somewhat severely on his connection with the theatre. "No man admitted more than he did the abilities of that right honourable gentleman, the elegant sallies of his thought, the gay effusions of his fancy, his dramatic turns, and his epigrammatic points; and if they were reserved for a proper stage, they would no doubt receive what the right honourable gentleman's abilities always did receive, the plaudits of the audience; and it would be his fortune *sui plausu gaudere theatri!* But this was not the proper scene for the exhibition of these elegances, and he therefore must beg leave to call the attention of the House to the serious consideration of the very important questions before them."

Sheridan in his reply proved himself quite equal to the occasion, and thus replied to the young Minister : " He need not comment upon that particular sort of personality which the right honourable gentleman had thought proper to introduce, the propriety, the taste, the gentlemanly point of it must have been obvious to the House. But," said Mr Sheridan, " let me assure the right honourable gentleman that I do now, and will at any time when he chooses to repeat this sort of allusion, meet it with the most sincere good humour. Nay, I will say more, flattered and encouraged by the right honourable gentleman's panegyric on my talents, if I ever again engage in the compositions he alludes to, I may be tempted to an act of presumption—to attempt an improvement on one of Ben Jonson's best characters — the character of the *Angry Boy* in the ' Alchymist.' "

BEING on a Parliamentary Committee on one occasion, Sheridan happened to enter the room when most of the members were present and seated, though business had not yet commenced ; when, perceiving that there was not another seat in the room, he asked with great readiness : "Will any gentleman *move* that I may *take the chair ?*"

—⁓∧∧∿—

LORD THURLOW attended the representation of *Pizarro*, but sunk into a deep sleep during Rolla's celebrated address to the Peruvians.

"Poor fellow," said Sheridan, on being informed of the circumstance, " I suppose he fancied he was on the Bench."

—⁓∧∧∿—

A PARTY of Sheridan's friends insisted on seeing him to his home when he was very tipsy. When they reached the street leading to the square in which he lived, he required them to leave him ; they did so, but after they had proceeded a short distance, turned round and saw him standing where they had left him, and using his umbrella like a person who is counting objects before him.

"What on earth, Sherry, are you about?" they asked.

"Do you not see," said he, "that all the houses in the square are going round and round? Well, I am waiting till mine comes by, and then I shall just step in."

THE Prince Regent having expatiated on the beauty of Dr Erasmus Darwin's opinion, that the reason why the bosom of a beautiful  woman possesses such a fascinating effect on man is because he derived from that source the first pleasurable sensations of his infancy, Sheridan very happily ridiculed the idea : "Such children, then, as are brought up by hand must needs be indebted for similar sensations to a very different object ; and yet, I believe, no man has ever felt any intense emotions of amatory delight at beholding a *pap-spoon !*"

TO a creditor who peremptorily required payment of the interest due on a long standing debt, Sheridan jocularly observed, "My dear sir, you know it is not my *interest* to pay the *principal;* nor is it my *principle* to pay the *interest.*"

A CREDITOR whom Sheridan had perpetually avoided, met him at last plump, coming out of Pall Mall from St James's Palace. There was no possibility of avoiding him, but Sheridan never lost his presence of mind.

"Oh," said he, "that's a beautiful mare you are on."

"D'ye think so!"

"Yes, indeed! How does she trot?"

The creditor, flattered, told him he should see, and immediately put her into full trotting pace. The instant he trotted off Sheridan turned into Pall Mall again, and was out of sight in a moment.

WHEN Pitt proposed a tax on female servants, Sheridan declared that it could be considered in no other light than as a bounty to bachelors, and a penalty upon propagation.

A MEMBER of Parliament having actually proposed a tax on tombstones as one which could meet with no objection, Sheridan replied, "that the only reason why the proposed tax could not be objected to was, because those out of whose property it was to be paid would know nothing of the matter, as they must be dead before the demand could be made; but then, after all, who knows but that it may not be rendered unpopular in being represented as a tax upon persons who, having paid the debt of nature, must prove that they have done so, by having the receipt engraved upon their tombs."

A N M.P., Mr Michael Angelo Taylor, had acquired the name of "the Chicken," by saying that he always delivered his legal opinion in the House, and elsewhere, with great humility, because he was young, and might, with propriety, call himself a *chicken in the profession of the law.* Sheridan in a humorous speech, which produced repeated peals of laughter, took notice of the diffidence of Mr Taylor, as connected with another observation of the same gentleman, "that he should then vote with the Opposition because they were in the right, but that in all probability he should never vote with them again;" thus presaging that for the future they would be always wrong.

"If such be his augury," said Sheridan, "I cannot help looking upon this chicken as a bird of ill-omen, and wish that he had continued side by side with the full-grown cock (alluding to Bearcroft), who will, no doubt, long continue to feed about the gates of the Treasury, to pick up those crumbs which are there plentifully scattered about to keep the chickens and full-grown fowls together."

BYRON, writing to Tom Moore, said :—
Perhaps you heard of a late answer of
Sheridan's to the watchman, who found him
bereft of that divine particle of air called
reason.   He, the watchman, who found Sherry

in the street fuddled and bewildered, and
almost insensible, said, " Who are *you*, sir?"
    No answer.
    "What's your name?"
    A hiccup.
    "What's your name?"
    Answer, in a slow, deliberate, impressive
tone, " *Wilberforce.*"

MRS CHOLMONDELEY asked to have an acrostic on her name. "An acrostic on your name," echoed Sheridan, "would be a formidable task; it must be so long that I think it should be divided into cantos."

It was during the same conversation that Sheridan said a lady should not write verses till she is past receiving them.

KELLY describes his appearance in the character of an Irishman in a Drury Lane Opera:—"My friend Johnstone took great pains to instruct me in the brogue, but I did not feel quite up to the mark; and, after all, it seems my vernacular phraseology was not the most perfect; for when the Opera was over, Sheridan came into the green-room and said, 'Bravo! Kelly; very well, indeed; upon my honour I never before heard *you speak such good English* in all my life.'"

SHERIDAN'S cool assurance never deserted him. Late one night, when in company with Challie, the wine-merchant, they were stopped by footpads. Sheridan quietly addressed them saying, "My friend can accommodate you, and as for myself, I'll tell you what I *can* do, I can give you my note of hand."

IN a speech on the existence of seditious practices in England, Sheridan gave the well-known and happy turn to the motto of the *Sun* newspaper, which was at that time known to be the organ of the alarmists :—There was one paper in particular, said to be the property of members of that House, and published and conducted under their immediate direction, which had for its motto a garbled part of a beautiful sentence, when it might with much more propriety, have assumed the whole—

> "*Solem quis dicere falsum Audeat? Ille etiam caecos instare tumultus Sæpe monet, fraudemque et operta tumescere bella.*"

IN the same speech Sheridan brilliantly ridiculed the people who took part in the prevailing panic :—The alarm had been brought forward in great pomp and form on Saturday morning. At night all the mail coaches were stopped; the Duke of Richmond stationed himself, among other curiosities, at the Tower; a great municipal officer, too, had made a discovery exceedingly beneficial to the people of this country. He meant the Lord Mayor of London, who had found out that there was at the King's Arms at Cornhill a Debating Society, where principles of the most dangerous tendency were propagated; where people went to buy

treason at sixpence a head ; where it was re-
tailed to them by the glimmering of an inch of
candle : and five minutes, to be measured by
the glass, were allowed to each traitor to
perform his part in overturning the State.

—∿∿∿—

K EMBLE and Sheridan were drinking together one evening, says Michael Kelly
in his *Reminiscences*, when Kemble complained
of the want of novelty at Drury
Lane Theatre, and said that he,
as manager, felt uneasy.

" My dear Kemble," said
Sheridan, " don't talk of griev-
ances now."

But Kemble still kept on, saying, " Indeed, we must seek for
novelty, or the theatre will sink—novelty, and
novelty alone, can prop it."

" Then," replied Sheridan, with a smile, " if
you want novelty, act Hamlet and have music
played *between your pauses*."

—∿∿∿—

C ONGREVE'S plays are, I own, somewhat
licentious, but it is barbarous to mangle
them ; they are like horses—when you deprive
them of their vice, they lose their vigour.

SHERIDAN made his appearance one day in a pair of new boots, which attracted the notice of some friends.

"Now, guess," said he, "how I came by these boots?"

Many *probable* guesses then took place. "No," said Sheridan, "no, you've not hit it, nor ever will—I bought them, *and paid for them!*"

IN a speech on the India Bill, Mr Scott (afterwards Lord Eldon) indulged in a licence of Scriptural parody, and had affected to discover the rudiments of the Bill in a chapter of the Book of Revelations,—Babylon being the East India Company, Mr Fox and his seven commissioners the Beast with the seven heads, and the marks on the hand and forehead, imprinted by the Beast upon those around him, meaning, evidently, he said, the peerages, pensions, and places distributed by the Minister.

In answering this strange sally of forensic wit, Sheridan quoted other passages from the same book, which, the reporter gravely assures us, "told strongly for the Bill," and which proved that Lord Fitzwilliam and his fellow-commissioners, instead of being the seven heads of the Beast, were seven angels, "clothed in pure and white linen!"

ON the success of a wildly romantic play by Monk Lewis, Sheridan was asked why he had desecrated the stage by such an abortion. —"Abortion, my dear friend, look to the treasury," was the reply. " I have long entertained the idea of converting *Romeo and Juliet* into a comic opera ; despatching the fiery Tybalt with the bravura ' The soldier

tired ' ; Mercutio to the lively air of ' Over the hills and far away ' ; and winding up with a grand scene in the graveyard, with the shades of the Capulets dancing among the tombstones to the solemn dirge of ' Where are you going, my pretty maid ? I am going a-milking, sir, she said.' Won't it be capital ? Lewis's success ensures my own."

L ET me have but the periodical press on my
side, and there should be nothing in this
country which I would not accomplish.

—∿∿∿—

W HEN someone told Sheridan that the
quantity of wine and spirits which he
drank would destroy the coat of his stomach,
he replied, "Well, then, my stomach must
just digest in its waistcoat."

—∿∿∿—

R OGERS and Sheridan were talking about
actors.

"Your admiration of Mrs Siddons is so
high," said Rogers, "that I wonder you never
made open love to her."

"To her!" exclaimed Sheridan, "to that
magnificent and appalling creature; I should
as soon have thought of making love to the
Archbishop of Canterbury."

—∿∿∿—

S IR JOHN HIPPISLEY, who had been
envoy at an Italian court, occupied himself
on his return to Parliament chiefly with the
Catholic question. On this subject he was
remarkable for supporting his speeches with

K

documents of the dryest and most antiquated species.

" I never hear that man speak," said a leader of the Opposition, "that I don't think I hear the ghost of some old Pope."

" Ay, of Pope Joan," added Sheridan.

—◦◦◦—

A DRAMA was presented to Sheridan, in which the characters amounted to no less than fifty-six.

"What's this? the new army list?" asked Sheridan.

" Nothing of the kind, sir," said the intro-ducer, "it is on an Irish story, and by an Irishman."

Sheridan glanced over a few leaves and saw that it was altogether inadmissible. " Tell my countryman that as a drama there can be no hope of its success, partly owing to the reduced population of London ; but it might be turned into a history of the Rebellion, and the list at the beginning would do for the muster at the levy *en masse.*"

MENTION having been made in his presence of a tax upon mile-stones, Sheridan said that such a tax would be unconstitutional,—as they were a race that could not meet to remonstrate.

IF the thought is slow to come, a glass of good wine encourages it, and, when it *does* come, a glass of good wine rewards it.

—⁓∿∿⁓—

" THE life of a manager of a theatre," Sheridan said, "was like the life of the ordinary at Newgate,—a constant superintendence of executions. The number of authors whom he was forced to extinguish was a perpetual literary massacre that made St Bartholomew's altogether shrink in comparison. Play-writing, singly, accounted for the employment of that immense multitude who drain away obscure years beside the inkstand, and haunt the streets with iron-moulded visages, and study-coloured clothes. It singly accounted for the rise of paper, which had exhausted the rags of England and Scotland, and had almost stripped off the last covering of Ireland. He had counted plays until calculation sank under the number ; and every rejected play of them all seemed like the clothes of a Spanish beggar, to turn into a living, restless, merciless, indefatigable progeny."

LADY ARGYLE asked Sheridan to explain "why our young men of birth persist in dressing, looking, and talking like boxers, grooms, and coachmen?"

"My dear Madam, I never had a turn for family secrets," replied Sheridan; "but I suspect *birth* to be the general cause."

—⁓⋁⋁⋁⋎—

WHEN Pitt's India Bill was brought up from Committee, it had twenty-one new clauses added, which were to be known by the letters from A to W. Sheridan said he hoped that some gentleman of ability would invent three more clauses for X, Y, and Z, to complete the alphabet, which would then render the bill a perfect hornbook for the use of the Minister, and the instruction of rising politicians.

—⁓⋁⋁⋁⋎—

DURING the "O. P. Row," when Sheridan was conversing with Kemble on the prospect of a speedy end being put to the popular disturbance, Kemble said, "that he had a *hope* of its conclusion from the trial of Clifford *v.* Brandon."

"For my part," replied Sheridan, "I see nothing in your *hope*, but an *aitch* and an O. P."

SHERIDAN'S parliamentary colleagues had brought in an extremely unpopular measure, on which they were defeated. He then said, that he had often heard of people knocking out their brains against a wall; but never before knew of anyone building a wall expressly for the purpose.

A CERTAIN noble lord having no less than nine nominees in the House of Commons, they were nicknamed the nine-pins. Burke made an able and satirical reply to a speech of one of these members, a reply that was received with a loud cheer. Fox entering the House at the moment, enquired of Sheridan the cause of it.

"Oh! nothing of any consequence," replied the wit, "only Burke knocking down one of the *nine-pins.*"

A CERTAIN Doctor was remarkable for his reluctance to contribute to public institutions. He was at length prevailed on to attend a charity sermon in Westminster. After the sermon, the plate was handed round the vestry. Fox and Sheridan were present.

"The Doctor has absolutely given his pound," said Fox.

"Then," said Sheridan, "he must think that he is going to die."

"Pooh!" replied Fox, "even Judas threw away twice the money."

"Yes; but how long was it before he was hanged?" retorted Sheridan.

—∿∿∿—

MICHAEL KELLY in his amusing *Reminiscences* has the following good story of Sheridan :—One evening after we had dined

together, I was telling him, that I was placed in a dilemma by a wine-merchant from Hockheim, who had been in London to receive orders for the sale of hock. I had commissioned him (as he offered me the wine at a cheap rate), to send me six dozen. Instead of six dozen, he had sent me *sixteen*. I was observing that it was a greater quantity than I could afford to keep, and expressed a wish to sell part of it.

"My dear Kelly," said Sheridan, "I would take it off your hands with all my heart, but I have not the money to pay for it; I will, however, give you an inscription to place over the door of your saloon: write over it, 'Michael Kelly, composer of wines and importer of music.'"

I thanked him, and said, "I will take the hint, sir, and be a composer of all wines, except old Sherry; for that is so notorious for its intoxicating and pernicious qualities that I should be afraid of poisoning my customers with it."

The above story has been told in many ways; but as I have written it here, is the fact. He owned I had given him a Roland for his Oliver, and very often used to speak of it in company.

—⁓ᴧᴧ⁓—

SHERIDAN'S maiden speech in the House of Commons was far from being successful. When it was over, he went to the reporters' gallery, and asked a friend, Woodfall, how he had succeeded. "I am sorry to say I do not think this is your line," said that candid friend, "you had much better have stuck to your former pursuits."

On hearing this, Sheridan rested his head on

his hands for a moment, and then vehemently
exclaimed, "It is in me, however, and, by God,
it shall come out."

DRURY LANE THEATRE was destroyed
by fire in February 1809. Sheridan was
in the House of Commons when he learned
that the fire had broken out. He hastened to
the scene, and with wonderful fortitude
witnessed the destruction of his property. He
sat at the Piazza Coffee-house taking some
refreshment; and on a friend remarking to
him how calmly he bore the ruin, Sheridan
merely said that surely a man might be allowed
to take a glass of wine at his own fireside.

LORD DERBY once applied at Drury Lane
to Mr Sheridan, with much dignity, for
the arrears of Lady Derby's (nee Farren) salary,
and vowed that he would not stir from the room
till it was paid.

"My dear Lord," said Sheridan, "this is
too bad; you have taken from us the brightest
jewel in the world, and you now quarrel with
us for a little of the dust she has left behind
her."

ON the Prince entering the Thatched-house Tavern and "raising his spirits *up* by pouring spirits *down*," Sheridan gave these impromptu lines—

"The Prince came in, and said 'twas cold,
    Then took a mighty rummer,
When *swallow* after *swallow* came,
    And then he swore 'twas summer."

—·∧∧∧·—

LORD BELGRAVE having clinched a speech in the House of Commons with a long Greek quotation, Sheridan, in reply, admitted the force of the quota-  tion so far as it went, "but," said he, "had the noble lord proceeded a little further and completed the passage, he would have seen that it applied the other way."

Sheridan then delivered some-thing, *ore rotundo*, which had all the ais, ois, ous, kon, and kos, that give the world assurance of a Greek quotation; upon which, Lord Belgrave very promptly and handsomely complimented the honourable member on his readiness of recollec-tion, and frankly admitted that the continuation of the passage had the tendency ascribed to it by Mr Sheridan, and that he had overlooked it at the moment when he gave his quotation.

On the breaking up of the House, Fox, who piqued himself on knowing *some* Greek, went up to Sheridan and asked him, "Sheridan, how came you to be so ready with that passage? It certainly is as you say, but I was not aware of it before you quoted it."

Sheridan had indeed successfully hoaxed the House, for his "quotation" was quite impromptu and entirely innocent of Greek!

THE scenery of Drury Lane was one evening on fire. The audience became alarmed and in an instant the confusion would have been dreadful. Suett rushed upstairs to Sheridan to tell him that the fire was extinguished, and that he would go and tell the house. "You fool," exclaimed Sheridan, "don't mention the word 'fire'; run and tell them that we have water enough to drown them all, and make a face."

The expedient succeeded; the house was calm in an instant, and was in a tumult of laughter only, at the strange grimaces of which Suett was such a master.

WHEN Sheridan lay upon his death-bed, his doctor thought that as a forlorn hope a certain operation might be performed. He

enquired of his patient, " Have you ever under-
gone an operation, Mr Sheridan?"

With a drollery which even pain and suffering
had not repressed, Sheridan replied, " Yes,—
when sitting for my portrait, or to have my
hair cut."

D URING the trial of Warren Hastings,
Sheridan in one of his speeches used a
metaphor which one of the opposing counsel

roughly handled afterwards. Sheridan replied,
" It was the first time in his life he had ever
heard of *special pleading* on a *metaphor*, or a
bill of indictment against a trope. But such
was the turn of the learned counsel's mind, that
when he attempted to be humorous, no jest
could be found, and, when serious, no fact was
visible."

RICHARDSON had set his mind upon going down to Bognor with Mr Sheridan on one particular occasion, because it happened that Lord Thurlow, with whom he was on terms of intimacy was staying there. "So," said Richardson, "nothing can be more delightful, what with my favorite diversion of sailing—my enjoyment of walking on the sand—the pleasure of arguing with Lord Thurlow, and taking my snuff by the seaside, I shall be in my glory."

"Well," said Sheridan, "down he went, full of anticipated joys. The first day, in stepping into the boat to go sailing, he tumbled down, and sprained his ankle, and was obliged to be carried into his lodgings, which had no view of the sea ; the following morning he sent for a barber to shave him, but there being no professional barber nearer than Chichester, he was forced to put up with a fisherman, who volunteered to officiate, and cut him severely just under his nose, which entirely prevented his taking snuff; and the same day at breakfast, eating prawns too hastily, he swallowed the head of one, horns and all, which stuck in his throat, and produced such pain and inflammation, that his medical advisers would not allow him to speak for three days. So thus ended, in four and twenty hours, his walking —his sailing—his snuff taking—and his arguments."

A DEBATE taking place as to the putting down of Sunday newspapers, Sheridan observed that there was an exception in the law in favour of selling mackerel on the Lord's day, and people might think stale news as bad as stale mackerel!

WHEN Sheridan was coming up to town in one of the public coaches for the purpose of canvassing Westminster, at the time when Paull was his opponent, he found himself in company with two Westminster electors. In the course of conversation one of them asked the other to whom he meant to give his vote. When his friend replied, "To Paull, certainly; for, though I think him but a shabby sort of a fellow, I would vote for anyone rather than that rascal Sheridan!"

"Do you know Sheridan?" asked the stranger.

"Not I, sir," answered the gentleman, "nor should I wish to know him."

The conversation dropped here; but when

the party alighted to breakfast, Sheridan called the other gentleman aside, and said—

" Pray who is that very agreeable friend of yours? He is one of the pleasantest fellows I ever met with, and should be glad to know his name."

" His name is Mr Richard Wilson ; he is an eminent lawyer, and resides in Lincoln's Inn Fields."

Breakfast over, the party resumed their seats in the coach ; soon after which Sheridan turned the discourse to the law. " It is," he said, " a fine profession.   Men may rise from it to the highest eminence in the State ; and it gives vast scope to the display of talent : many of the most virtuous and noble characters recorded in our history have been lawyers ; I am sorry, however, to add, that some of the greatest rascals have also been lawyers ; but of all the rascals of lawyers I ever heard of, the greatest is one Wilson, who lives in Lincoln's Inn Fields."

" I am Mr Wilson," said the gentleman.

" And I am Mr Sheridan," was the reply.

The jest was instantly seen ; they shook hands, and instead of voting against the facetious orator, the lawyer exerted himself warmly in promoting his election.

SHERIDAN having very successfully adapted Kotzebue's play of *The Stranger*, a friend rebuked him for not employing his great talents to more legitimate purposes than that of adapting foreign sentimentality, with its tinsel embellishments, to the English stage.

He replied in these lines of Dr Johnson's—

" ' The drama's laws the drama's patrons give,
And those who live to please must please to live.'

Kotzebue and German sausages are the order of the day."

—⁄\⁄\⁄\⁄—

BEING stopped one night by a footpad, who demanded his purse, Sheridan, offering no resistance, merely said, " My purse, well, here it is : if you can find anything in it, it is more than I can ; therefore, I entreat you, let us go halves in the finding."

—⁄\⁄\⁄\⁄—

A FRIEND remonstrating with Sheridan on the instability of his means of supporting his costly establishment in Orchard Street, he tartly replied, "My dear friend, *it is my means.*"

—⁄\⁄\⁄\⁄—

AN admirer of Sheridan's was anxious that he should write a tragedy, but the dramatist replied that there were quite enough of *comedies of that class*, and he would not add to their number.

BEING upon one occasion sorely pressed by a needy creditor, who said that he had a heavy payment to make *to-morrow*, Sheridan replied to his entreaties, "Well, be it to-morrow, it is a favourite day of mine to which I refer many of my obligations ; and when to-morrow comes, I hope we shall both be prepared to pass our accounts to our mutual satisfaction."

—◦◦◦—

SHERIDAN, who was no sportsman, visited an old sportsman in Ireland, and gave afterwards an amusing account of his experience. In order to avoid the imputation of being a  downright ignoramus, he was under the necessity of taking a gun, and at the dawn of day setting forth in pursuit of game. Unwilling to expose his want of skill, he took an opposite course to that of his friend, and was accompanied by a gamekeeper, provided with a bag to receive the birds which might fall victims to his attacks, and a pair of excellent pointers. The game-keeper was a true Pat, and possessed all those arts of *blarney* for which his country-men are noted ; and thinking it imperative on him to be particularly attentive to his master's friend, he lost no opportunity of praising his prowess. The first covey (and the birds were abundant) rose within a few yards of the states-man's nose, but the noise they made was so unexpected, that he waited till they were out of harm's way before he fired.

Pat, who was on the look out, expressed his surprise, and immediately observed, " Faith, sir, I see you know what a gun is : it 's well you wasn't nearer, or them chaps would be sorry you ever came into the country."

Sheridan reloaded and went on, but his second shot was not more successful.

" Oh," cried Pat, " what an escape ! I 'll be bound you rumpled some of their feathers ! "

The gun was loaded again, and on went the orator ; but the third shot was as little effective as the two former.

" Hah," exclaimed Pat, although astonished at so palpable a miss, " I 'll lay a thirteen you don't come near us to-day again ; master was too near you to be pleasant."

So he went on, shot after shot, and always had something to say to console poor Sheridan, who was not a little amused at his ingenuity. At last, on their return home, without a bird in the bag, Sheridan perceived a covey quietly feeding on the other side of a hedge, and un-willing to give them a chance of flight, he resolved to have a slap at them on the ground. He did so, but, to his mortification, they all flew away untouched.

L

Pat, whose excuses were now almost exhausted, still had something to say, and he exclaimed joyfully, looking at Sheridan very significantly, " By Jasus ! you made them lave that, anyway ! " and with this compliment to his sportsmanlike qualities, Sheridan says he closed his morning's amusement, laughing heartily at his companion, and rewarding him with a half-crown for his patience and encouragement.

SHERIDAN was told by a friend that his enemies took pleasure in speaking ill of him, on account of his favouring an obnoxious

tax which his party were about to force through the House. " Well, let them," he replied ; " it is but fair that they should have some *pleasure* for their money."

WHEN Miss Farren, the original Lady
Teazle, retired from the stage to
become the Countess of Derby, Sheridan paid
her a happy compliment. He approached her
in the green room, surrounded by her friends
and admirers, and, raising her hand with some
emotion to his lips, breathed into her ear,—
"God bless you : *Lady Teazle is no more, and
the 'School for Scandal' has broke up for the
holidays.*"

ON the re-opening of Drury Lane Theatre
after the burning, Whitbread had written
an address, in which like the other addresses,
there were many allusions to the Phœnix.
Sheridan remarked upon this that Whitbread
made more of this bird than any of them ;
he entered into particulars, and described its
wings, back, and tail ; in short, it was a poul-
terer's description of a Phœnix.

PALMER, the original Joseph Surface, whose
real character was quite in keeping with
the assumed one, had left Drury Lane Theatre
and started in opposition, but soon came to
grief, and was glad to get back. The first
time the returned actor met Sheridan after
his escapade, it was with the air of a Joseph
Surface. With a white pocket-handkerchief in

his hand, his eyes upturned, his hand upon his heart, he began, " Mr Sheridan, if you could but know at this moment what I feel *here!*"

" Stop, Jack," broke in the manager, " you forget that *I wrote it!*"

—◦◦◦—

IN Sheridan's Westminster election contest, Paull, his antagonist, who was the son of a tailor, envious of the brilliant uniform and more brilliant decorations of Sir S. Hood, observed with some spleen, " that if he had chosen he might have appeared before the electors with such a coat himself."

" Yes, and you might have made it, too," retorted Sheridan.

—◦◦◦—

ALLUDING to the stoppage of cash pay- ments at the Bank, in a committee of which Mr Bragge was chairman, Sheridan said that the conduct of the Chancellor of the Exchequer reminded him of an old proverb. The report of the committee was very favour- able ; but still the Bank must be kept under confinement : " Brag is a good dog," says the Minister, " but Holdfast is a better" : and the Bank must be kept under his tutelage until he finds it convenient to set the directors at liberty.

TALKING with a friend who had said that Pitt was a very extraordinary man, Sheridan answered, "He *is* an extraordinary man, and the more we press him, the more he shines."

—◇◇◇—

ON being asked by a young Member of Parliament how he first succeeded in establishing his fame as an orator, Sheridan observed :—"Why, sir, it was easily effected. After I had been in St Stephen's Chapel a few days, I found that four-fifths of the House were composed of country squires and great fools ; my first effort, therefore, was by a lively sally, or an ironical remark to make them laugh ; that laugh effaced the recollection of what had been urged in opposition to my view of the subject from their stupid pates, and then I whipped in an argument, and had all the way clear before me."

—◇◇◇—

LORD JOHN RUSSELL, in recounting Sheridan's joke to Tarleton, says, "Any one might think the wit poor (although I do not agree with them), but the joke is clear enough. ' I was on a horse, and now I'm on an elephant' (*i.e.* ' I was high above others, but now I am much higher'). 'You were on an ass, and now you're on a mule,' said Sheridan (*i.e.*, 'You *were* stupid and now you're obstinate'). For quick repartee in conversation there are few things better."

SOME one was complaining of an ugly house built by D'Arblay just near them at Leatherhead, when Sheridan said, "Oh, you know we can easily get rid of that, we can pack it off out of the country under the Alien Act."

DURING the great trial of Warren Hastings, Sheridan was making one of his speeches, when, having observed Gibbon among the audience, he took occasion to refer to the " luminous author of the *Decline and Fall!*" A friend afterwards reproached him for flattering Gibbon.

" Why, what did I say of him?" asked Sheridan.

" You called him the luminous author of the *Decline and Fall.*

" Luminous! oh, of course I meant voluminous."

ONE of Sheridan's retorts on Pitt, "the heaven-born Minister," showed singular readiness of allusion and presence of mind when they were least to be expected. One night Sheridan entered the House drunk ; Pitt, observing his condition, proposed to postpone some discussion in which Sheridan was concerned, in consideration of the peculiar state of the honourable member. Sheridan upon this fired ; and the instant his self-possession returned, rose, and remarked that in the history of that House, he believed, but one instance of the disgraceful conduct insinuated by the honourable member had occurred. There was but one example of members having entered that House in a state of temporary disqualification for its duties, and that example, however discreditable to the parties, could not perhaps be deplored, as it had given rise to a pleasant epigram. The honourable member on the Treasury Bench would correct him, if he misquoted the words. Two gentlemen, the one blind drunk, the other seeing double, staggered into the House, arm in arm, and thus communicated their parliamentary views to each other—

> " I can't see the Speaker,
>   Pray, Hal, do you?"
> " Not see the Speaker, Bill !
>   Why I see *two*."

Henry Dundas and Pitt himself were the heroes of the tale.

ON Lord Lauderdale telling Sheridan that he had heard an excellent joke which he would repeat, Sheridan stopped him saying, "Pray don't, my dear Lauderdale; in your mouth a joke is no laughing matter."

DURING Sheridan's management, Thomas Holcroft had produced a play which he offered to Covent Garden, saying, that it would

make Drury nothing but a "splendid ruin." Afterwards, when he offered a play to Sheridan, Sheridan retorted, "Come, come, Holcroft, it would be rather too bad to make me the instrument of accomplishing your own prediction."

SHERIDAN being at one time a good deal plagued by an old maiden relation of his always going out to walk with him, said one day that the weather was bad and raining; to which the old lady answered, on the contrary, it had cleared up.

"Yes," said Sheridan, "it has cleared up enough for *one*, but not enough for *two*."

—·/\/\·—

LORD ERSKINE declared in a large party, where Sheridan also was present, that "a wife was only a tin canister tied to one's tail," on which Sheridan presented Lady Erskine with these lines—

" Lord Erskine, at women presuming to rail.
  Calls a wife a 'tin canister tied to one's tail!'
  And the fair Lady Anne, while the subject he carries
    on,
  Seems hurt at his Lordship's degrading comparison :
  But wherefore degrading? Considered aright—
  A canister 's polished. and useful. and bright.
  And should dirt its original purity hide.
  That 's the fault of the puppy. to whom it is tied."

—√√√√—

"THE right honourable gentleman," said Sheridan, replying to Mr Dundas in the House of Commons, "is indebted to his memory for his jests, and to his imagination for his facts."

WHEN perusing *Vortigern*, the forged play ascribed to Shakespeare, Sheridan remarked, turning to Ireland the elder (father of the forger), "This is rather strange ; for though you are acquainted with my opinion of Shakespeare, yet be it as it may, he certainly always wrote *poetry.*"

—⌁⌁⌁—

THE orator very happily illustrated the style of a bill to remedy the defects of bills already in being by comparing it to the plan of a simple, but very ingenious moral tale, that had often afforded him amusement in his early days, under the title of the  *House that Jack Built.* First, then, comes in a bill, imposing a tax ; and then comes in a bill to amend that bill for imposing a tax ; and then comes in a bill to explain the bill that amended the bill for imposing a tax ; next a bill to remedy the defects of a bill for explaining the bill that amended the bill for imposing a tax ; and so on *ad infinitum.*

—⌁⌁⌁—

LOUNGING towards Whitehall, Sheridan met George Rose coming out of St Margaret's.

"Any mischief on foot, George, that you have been at church?"

"No; I have been getting a son christened; I have called him William Pitt."

"William Pitt!" echoed Sheridan. "A *rose* by any other name would smell as sweet."

SHERIDAN having said of one of the members of the Cabinet that having three places in a most gentlemanly administration, he must be three times as much a gentleman as his colleagues. The member referred to, then recently married, very gravely assured the House that his situation was not to be envied—that every morning when he got up, and every night when he went to rest, he had a task to perform almost too great for human powers. Sheridan instantly retorted that he himself would be very happy to relieve Dundas from the fatigues of the *Home* Department!

POLESDEN, Sheridan's residence, was near to Leatherhead, respecting which there had been much punning at his expense. When he was told of this in the country, he replied that on his return to town he would *get out of their debts*.

"What will you pay them?" asked a friend.

"Oh! I'll give them a *strapping!*"

IN the year 1801 Pitt had resigned his post as
Minister, and was succeeded by Addington ;
all the other Ministers retaining the positions.
Sheridan thus humorously ridiculed the arrange-
ment :—When the ex-minister quitted office,
almost all the *subordinate* ministers kept their
places.   How was it that the whole family did
not move together?   Had he only one covered
wagon to carry friends and goods? or has he

left directions behind him that they may know
where to call?   I remember a fable of Aristo-
phanes', which is translated from Greek into
decent English.   I mention this for the country
gentlemen.   It is of a man that sat so long on
a seat — about as long, perhaps, as the ex-
minister did on the Treasury Bench—that he
grew to it.   When Hercules pulled him off, he
left all the sitting part of the man behind.   The
House can make the allusion.

THE son of Sheridan, Tom, who was expecting to get into Parliament, said on one occasion to his father, " I think that many men who are called great patriots in the House of Commons are great humbugs. For my own part, if I get into Parliament, I will pledge myself to no party; but write upon my forehead in legible character, ' to be let.' "

" And under that, Tom," said his father, " write ' unfurnished.' "

—∿∿∿—

SHERIDAN was accosted one day by a gentlemanly-looking elderly man who had forgotten the name of the street to which he wished to get, when the following dialogue took place :—

" Sir, I wish to go to a street the name of which I have forgotten. It is a very uncommon name—pray, sir, can you tell me of any such street near ? "

" Perhaps, sir, you mean John Street ? " enquired Sheridan.

" No ; it is a street with an unusual name."

" It can't be Charles Street ? "

" It is not a common name," said the stranger a little testily, " it has the most unusual name for a street."

" Surely, sir," said Sheridan, " you are not looking for King Street ? "

" I tell you, sir, it is a street with a very odd name."

"Bless me, sir," said Sheridan, as though struck by a happy thought, "it is not Queen Street, is it?"

"Queen Street!—no, no! it is a curious sort of name I tell you."

" I wish, sir, I could assist you," continued Sheridan ; "let me think. It may be Oxford Street?"

"Sir, for heaven's sake," exclaimed the irate stranger, "think of what I told you, that it is a street with anything but a common name ; everybody knows Oxford Street."

"Perhaps, sir, the street has no name after all," ventured Sheridan, in all seriousness, as though offering a likely solution.

"No name, sir!—Why, I tell you it has—confound the name!"

"Really, sir," went on Sheridan, "I am very sorry that I am unable to assist you—but let me suggest Piccadilly."

The stranger could no longer restrain his irritation, but bounced away, exclaiming "Oh, damn it, what a thick-headed fellow it is!"

Sheridan, calling to him, and bowing as he turned, replied, "Sir, I envy you your admirable memory," and then walked on, thoroughly enjoying his joke.

—∿∿∿—

" STEAL! to be sure they will," said Sheridan of some plagiarists, "and, egad! serve your best thoughts as gipsies do stolen children—disfigure them to make them pass for their own."

DURING the Westminster election contest, owing to the tactics of some of Sheridan's supporters, one of the voters called out that he should withdraw his countenance from him.

"Take it away at once—take it away at once!" cried Sheridan, "it is the most villainous looking countenance I ever beheld."

" BY the silence that prevails," said Sheridan, on entering a room full of guests, " I conclude that Lauderdale has been making a joke."

WHEN the Duke of York was obliged to retreat before the French, Sheridan gave as a toast, " The Duke of York and his brave *followers.*"

RECOMMENDED to a course of sea-bathing, Sheridan objected, saying that pickles did not agree with him.

SPEAKING in Parliament, Sheridan compared a tax-bill to a ship built in a dock-
yard, which was found to be defective every
voyage, and consequently was obliged to un-
dergo a new repair; first it was to be caulked,
then to be new planked, then to be new ribbed,
then again to be covered ; then, after all these
expensive alterations, the vessel was obliged to
be broken up and rebuilt.

———◦◦◦———

IN a pantomime which Sheridan wrote for
Drury Lane Theatre, there was a practical
joke—where in pulling off a man's boot, the leg
was pulled off with it, which the famous Delpini
laid claim to as his own, and publicly complained
of Sheridan's having stolen it from him. Sheridan said it was claimed as literary property,
being *in usum Delpini*.

———◦◦◦———

SHERIDAN, the first time he met Tom after
his marriage, was seriously angry with him,
and told him that he had made his will and cut
him off with a shilling.

Tom said he was, indeed, very sorry, and
immediately added, "You don't happen to
have the shilling about you now, sir, do
you?"

A LONG-WINDED member of Parliament stopped in the midst of a tedious oration to take a glass of water. Sheridan immediately "rose to a point of order." Everybody wondered what the point of order could be.

"What is it?" asked the Speaker.

"I think, sir," said Sheridan, "that it is out of order for a windmill to go by water."

ONE of school-day *mots* attributed to Sheridan is this:—A gentleman having a remarkably long visage was one day riding by

the school, when he heard young Sheridan say, "That gentleman's face is longer than his life." Struck by the strangeness of the remark, he turned his horse's head, and requested the boy's meaning.

"Sir," replied he, "I meant no offence in the world, but I have read in the Bible at school, that a man's life is but a span, and I am sure your *face* is double that length."

M

LORD ELLENBOROUGH (then Mr Law) had once to cross-examine Sheridan. He commenced thus : " Pray, Mr Sheridan, do answer my questions, without point or epigram."

" You say true, Mr Law," retorted the wit, " your questions are without point or epigram."

—◇◇◇—

SAID Beau Brummel : " My brain, Sherry, is swimming with being up all night—how can I cure it? I am not myself this morning."

" Then what are you?" asked Sheridan. " But no matter. You have mistaken your complaint ; there can be no swimming in a *caput mortuum.*"

—◇◇◇—

DAVID HUME and Sheridan were crossing the water, when, a high gale arising, the philosopher seemed under great apprehension lest he should go to the bottom.

" Why," said Sheridan, " that will suit your genius to a tittle ; for my part, I care only for skimming on the surface."

—◇◇◇—

BEING told that the lost tribes of Israel had been found, Sheridan said he was glad to hear it, as he had nearly exhausted the other ten.

GEORGE ROSE of the Treasury was talking to an individual in the House of Commons. Sheridan was standing close to him when a friend came up, and asked, " What news, to-day?—anything afloat?"

"Nothing, my dear fellow, nothing, except the rumour of a great defalcation in the Treasury—mind, *sub Rosa!*" replied Sheridan loud enough to have been heard all round.

SHERIDAN once succeeded admirably in entrapping a noisy member who was in the habit of interrupting every speaker with cries of " Hear, hear!" He took an opportunity to allude to a well-known political character of the times, whom he represented as a person who wished to play the rogue, but had only sense enough to play the fool.

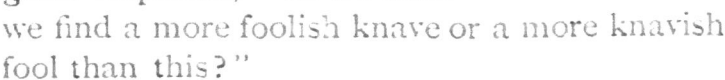

" Where," exclaimed Sheridan, in continuation, and with great emphasis, " where shall we find a more foolish knave or a more knavish fool than this?"

" Hear, hear!" was instantly bellowed from the accustomed bench. The wicked wit bowed, thanked the gentleman for his ready reply to the question, and sat down amid convulsions of laughter from all but their unfortunate subject.

—◇◇◇—

TOM SHERIDAN once mentioned to his father that he thought of going down a coal mine.

"Go down a coal mine!" exclaimed the other, astonished, "what is your reason?"

"Oh," said Tom, "I think it would be rather a nice thing to say that one had been down a pit."

"Well, but you can *say* so," said his father.

—◇◇◇—

ALMOST to the very last, Sheridan preserved his readiness of wit and pleasantry. A solicitor who had been much favoured in wills, waited on him, and after he had gone another caller came in, to whom Sheridan said, "My friends have been very kind in calling upon me and offering their services in their respective ways. Dick W., for instance, has just been here with his will-making face."

—◇◇◇—

IN consequence of a continued bout of dissipation, Sheridan was taken ill. He sent for a doctor, who prescribed rigid abstinence.

Calling some time after, the medical man asked his patient if he was attending to his advice, and was answered in the affirmative.

"Right," said the doctor; "'tis the only way to secure you length of days."

"I do not doubt it," said Sheridan, "for

these three last days have been the longest to me in my life."

BURKE'S melodramatic flinging of the dagger on the floor of the House of Commons was a complete failure, and produced nothing but a smothered laugh, and a joke from Sheridan,—"The gentleman has brought us the *knife*, but where is the *fork?*"

ONE of the Scotch Members of Parliament asked Sheridan how he got rid of the Irish brogue, as he wished to avoid his own Scotch accent.

"My dear fellow," said Sheridan, "don't attempt any such thing. The House listens to you now because they don't understand you; but if you become intelligible, they will be able to take your measure!"

SOON after the Irish members were admitted into the House of Commons on the Union in 1801, one of them, in the middle of his maiden speech, thus addressed the chair:—"And now, *my dear* Mr Speaker."

This excited loud laughter. As soon as it had somewhat subsided, Sheridan observed, "that the honourable member was perfectly in order; for thanks to the Ministers, nowadays, *everything is dear.*"

A LOQUACIOUS author, after babbling some time about his piece to Sheridan, said, "Sir, I fear I have been intruding on your attention."

"Not at all, I assure you," replied he; "I was thinking of *something else.*"

SHERIDAN was down at Brighton one day, when Fox (the manager) desirous of showing him some civility, took him all over the theatre and exhibited its beauties.

"There, Mr Sheridan," said Fox, who combined twenty occupations without being clever in any, "I built and painted all these boxes, and I painted all these scenes."

"Did you?" said Sheridan, surveying them rapidly. "Well, I should not, I am sure, have known you were a Fox by your *brush*."

—⁓w⁓—

CLIFFORD, a lawyer who had made some strong comments upon his political conduct, was once handled by Sheridan with considerable irony. To these comments Sheridan replied :—"As to the lawyer who has honoured me with so much abuse, I do not know how to answer him, as I am no great proficient in the language or manners of St Giles's. But one thing I can say of him, and it is in his favour. I hardly expect you will believe me, but I pledge you my 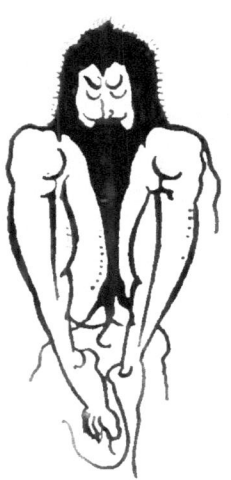 word that once, if not twice, but most assuredly once, I did meet him in the company of gentlemen."

AFTER witnessing the first representation of
a dog-piece by Reynolds, called the *Caravan*, Sheridan suddenly entered the green-
room, as it was imagined, to congratulate the
author.

" Where is he ? where is my guardian angel ? "
he anxiously enquired.

" Here I am," answered Reynolds.

" Pooh ! " replied Sheridan, " I don't mean
you, I mean *the dog*."

—◦◦◦—

SHERIDAN was once asked by an acquaintance, " How is it that your name has not
an O prefixed to it ? Your family is Irish, and
no doubt illustrious."

" No family," answered Sheridan, " has a
better right to an O than our family ; for, in
truth, we *owe* everybody."

—◦◦◦—

" WHY do we honour ambition and despise
avarice, while they are both but the
desire of possession ? " enquired a friend of
Sheridan.

" Because," answered he, " the one is natural,
the other artificial ; the one the sign of mental
health, the other of mental decay ; the one
appetite, the other disease."

WHEN Sheridan was asked which performer
he liked best in a certain piece, he replied,
"The prompter; for I saw less and heard more
of him than anyone else."

—◦∿∿◦—

PITT having introduced his Sinking Fund
into the House of Commons, Sheridan
ridiculed it, saying that "at present
it was clear there was no surplus;
and the only means which suggested
themselves to him were, a loan of a
million for the special purpose—for the right honourable gentleman might say,
with the person in the
comedy, "*If you won't lend
me the money, how can I pay you?*"

—◦∿∿◦—

IN a large party, one evening, the conversation turned upon young men's allowances
at college. Tom Sheridan lamented the ill-
judging parsimony of many parents in that
respect.

"I am sure, Tom," said his father, "you
need not complain; I always allowed you eight
hundred a year."

"Yes, father," replied Tom, " I must confess
you *allowed* it ; but then it was never paid."

LADY CRAVEN having quarrelled with Sheridan, said, that she kept up her resentment as long as she was able, until he made her laugh one night in a crowd coming out of the Opera House.

"We were squeezed near one another by chance, and he said, 'For God's sake! Lady Craven, don't tell anybody I am a thief; for you know very well, if you do, everybody will believe it!'"

—◊◊◊—

THE disputatious humour of one of his friends, Richardson by name, was once turned to good account by Sheridan in a very characteristic manner. Having had a hackney coach in employ for about five or six hours and not being provided with the means to pay for it Sheridan happened to espy Richardson in the street, and at once proposed to take him in the coach part of his way. The offer was accepted and Sheridan lost no time in starting a conversation on which he knew that his companion was sure to become argumentative and animated. Having by well-managed contradiction brought him to the proper pitch of excitement, Sheridan affected to grow impatient and angry himself; at length saying that "he could not think of staying in the same coach with a person that would use such language," he pulled the check-string and desired the coachman to let him out. Richardson, wholly occupied with the argument, and regarding the retreat of his opponent as an acknowledgment of defeat, still pressed his point, and even shouted "more last words" through the coach window after Sheridan, who, walking quietly home, left the poor disputant responsible for the heavy fare of the coach.

IN the debate on an India Control Bill, Sheridan said,—He remembered that the India Board had been compared to seven doctors and eight apothecaries administering to the health of one poor patient; but their prescriptions were more palatable than the dose now mixing by the learned Doctor of Control (Dundas), who, in the true spirit of quackery, desires his patient to take it,—that he has no occasion to confine himself at home, but may safely go about his business as usual. This sovereign remedy would, no doubt, soon be advertised under the popular name of "*Scots pills for all sorts of Oriental ills.*"

A NUMEROUS party was assembled at the mansion of a northern squire. Among them was Sheridan and a wealthy young heir

belonging to a neighbouring county. The youth prided himself on the accident of his birth, and on his consequent acquisition of riches. During the early part of the day the stripling sneered at poverty, and spoke slightingly of authors, actors, and other classes of the community who afford occupation and amusement to thousands who would be otherwise devoured by *ennui*, or seek excitement in vicious pleasures.

Sheridan was naturally displeased at the want of tact, taste, and feeling in the young plutocrat, and quietly waited an opportunity of making him feel the edge of his keen rebuke. At dinner there were twenty guests. Sheridan sat on the left hand at the bottom of the table, the youth on the right at the top, so that they were at opposite angles, and the whole party were so placed as to hear what passed from either of them.

The youth talked much of all that concerned him ; he gave accounts of the wonderful leaping of his favourite hunter ; of the distance at which his new double barrelled gun killed a wild duck ; of the extraordinary staunchness of a cross-bred setter ; of his dexterity in catching a salmon with a single hair ; of his prowess in London, &c. &c., to the number of eighteen remarkable circumstances.

After the removal of the second course silence ensued. Sheridan availed himself of this

moment, and thus addressed the youth—his
voice commanding the rest to silence—"Sir,
at the distance at which I sit from you, I did
not hear with accuracy the whole of your
interesting anecdotes ; permit me to ask you—

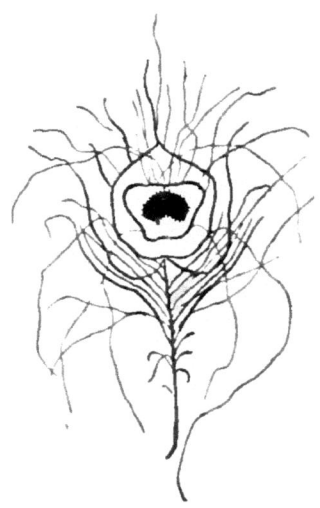

whose hunter performed those extraórdinary
leaps ? "

The youth promptly replied, " Mine, sir."

Sheridan continued, " But whose gun was it
that killed so far ? "

Again the youth answered, " Mine, sir."

" Whose setter was so staunch ? "

" Mine, sir," repeated the victim.

" Who caught the salmon did you say ? "

" I did," was faintly answered.

Sheridan was inexorable, and continued, with
the utmost politeness of manner until he had
exhausted the whole eighteen items ; and then

drily said, "So you were the chief *actor* in every anecdote, and the *author* of them all. Is it not rather impolitic to despise your own professions?"

The youth left the mansion the following day —cured, it is to be hoped of his illiberality, his egotism, and his boastfulness.

—∿∿∿—

ONE day, when quite a boy, Tom Sheridan, who had evidently been reading about the Necessarians, suddenly asked his father, "Pray, my good father, did you ever do anything in a state of perfect indifference, without a motive, I mean, of some kind or other?"

Sheridan, who saw what was coming, and had no relish for metaphysical discussion, replied, "Yes, certainly."

"Indeed?" said Tom.

"Yes, indeed."

"What, total indifference; total, entire, thorough indifference?"

"Yes, total, entire, thorough indifference."

"Well, now then, my dear father, tell me what it is that you can do with (mind) total, entire, thorough indifference."

"Why I can listen to you, Tom," said Sheridan.

—∿∿∿—

TOM was recommended by his father to take a wife, when he quietly asked, "Whose wife, sir?"

TOM SHERIDAN was, however, emphatically the son of his father. He was complaining to him once that his pockets were empty, when the elder Sheridan laconically replied, "Try the highway."

"I have," answered Tom, "but I made a bad hit. I stopped a caravan full of passengers, who assured me they had not a farthing, for they all belonged to Drury Lane Theatre and could not get a single penny of their salary."

—◦◦◦—

ON another and similar occasion, too, the younger Sheridan proved a witty match for his father. Sheridan had a cottage near Hounslow Heath. Tom being short of money asked his father to let him have some cash. "I have none," was the reply.

"Be the consequence what it may, money I must have," said Tom.

"If that is so, you will find a case of loaded pistols upstairs, and a horse ready saddled in the stable; the night is dark, and you are within half a mile of Hounslow Heath."

"I understand what you mean," said Tom; "but I tried that last night. I unluckily stopped Peake, your treasurer, who told me that you had been beforehand with him, and had robbed him of every sixpence in the world."

Lightning Source UK Ltd.
Milton Keynes UK
UKHW04f0611191018

330818UK00001B/154/P